Equity, Efficiency, and the U.S. Corporation Income Tax

Equity, Efficiency, and the U.S. Corporation Income Tax

J. Gregory Ballentine

American Enterprise Institute for Public Policy Research
Washington, D.C.

Library of Congress Cataloging in Publication Data

Ballentine, J   Gregory.
 Equity, efficiency, and the U. S. corporation income tax.

 (Studies in tax policy) (AEI studies ; 263)
 Bibliography: p.
 1. Corporations—Taxation—United States.   2. Tax incidence—
United States.   I. Title.   II. Series.   III. Series: American
Enterprise Institute for Public Policy Research.   AEI studies ; 263.
HJ4653.C7B34   336.2′43′0973   79-26226
ISBN 0-8447-3366-0

AEI Studies 263

Printed in the United States of America

CONTENTS

ACKNOWLEDGMENTS

This book has benefited from the comments of a number of persons. I would particularly like to thank Edgar Browning, O. H. Brownlee, Mervyn King, Charles E. McLure, Jr., John Owen, Rudolph Penner, and Wayne Thirsk. I am solely responsible for any errors or omissions that remain.

INTRODUCTION

The corporation income tax is probably the most controversial of the major revenue sources of the federal government. As long as opinions differ as to what constitutes an equitable distribution of the burden of government taxes and at what cost, in reduced growth or inefficiency, gains in equity are to be purchased, tax policies will be a source of controversy. But such controversy is compounded in the case of the corporation income tax because economists are uncertain about the actual effects of that tax on the distribution of income, the allocation of resources, and economic growth.

As will be discussed in succeeding chapters, some analysts have argued that the corporation income tax causes prices to rise and is largely borne by the consumer. If this is so, the tax is slightly regressive or proportional. Others have argued that the tax is borne by stockholders in the short run but that in the long run, through adjustments in investment, the burden is diffused among all capitalists and is even borne in part by labor. Both sets of conclusions have stemmed from analysis in which the adjustments in financial policy that corporations may make in order to avoid the tax have been ignored. Recently it has been shown that, under certain extreme assumptions, corporations may be able to adjust their financial policies so that the tax has no effect in the economy except that of reducing the wealth of those who owned stock when the tax was imposed or increased.

In spite of the wide range of opinion on specific aspects of the corporation income tax, two broad, significant conclusions can be drawn from the bulk of recent literature:

- The burden of the corporation income tax is diffused throughout the economy; it is shared by consumers, capitalists, and laborers. Precisely how much of the burden is borne by each group is unclear at present and may remain so. Consequently, it is virtually impossible to argue that the tax meets any well-defined equity goals of society.

• The corporation income tax imposes a significant cost on society. This cost arises from the distorting effect of the tax on capital markets or, if it is shifted in the short run, on product markets. In the former instance the distortion manifests itself as a capital shortage in the corporate sector of the economy, while in the latter it is manifested as a wedge between the marginal costs of corporations and the prices that they charge.

Even though these two conclusions are not consistent with all the literature, they will serve as a useful frame of reference for our examination of current opinion about the corporation income tax. Clearly, if these two conclusions are correct, there is a strong case for reduced reliance on that tax.[1]

In the first chapter of this study the rationale of a tax on corporation profits in addition to the personal income tax is examined briefly. Chapters 2, 3, and 4 deal with the question, Who actually bears the burden of the extra tax on corporate income? In the first two of these chapters it is assumed that firms do not adjust their financial policies—particularly their combination of debt and equity finance—in response to the corporation income tax. The recent literature, in which it is explicitly recognized that the tax falls only on equity profits and that corporations can avoid much of the impact of the tax by adjusting their financial policies, will be reviewed in Chapter 4.

In Chapter 5 we turn from the distributional effects of the corporate tax to its effects on efficiency, which operate through the misallocation of resources among different sectors of the economy at any one time as well as through the misallocation of consumption over time. Both of these give rise to a capital shortage in the corporate sector of our economy.

In the last chapter we will deal with a special topic that is, unfortunately, quite relevant to the economy today—inflation and the corporation income tax. Inflation exacerbates many of the problems associated with the taxation of corporate income.

Before beginning to discuss those issues, it is important to mention certain aspects of corporate taxation in the United States today. Since its imposition, the corporate tax has undergone considerable evolution. Initially it was a proportional tax on all equity profits,

---

[1] Ideally, reduced reliance upon the corporation income tax would not come about by simply removing the tax but would involve integrating corporate and personal income taxes. The issue of tax integration is explained and discussed briefly in Chapter 1.

though small exemptions applied in some years. In 1935 graduation was introduced, and the present tax is a graduated tax, with a rate of 17 percent on the first $25,000 rising in four steps to 46 percent on profits above $100,000. In spite of this progressivity in the rate structure, we will speak of a single corporate tax rate throughout the discussion. Since the bulk of corporate profits are subject to the statutory rate of 46 percent, this simplification is not of great significance.[2]

Two more recent and important changes in our corporation income tax system are the introduction of accelerated depreciation in 1954 and the investment tax credit which has been used off and on since 1962. Accelerated depreciation allows firms to deduct from income an overstatement of true depreciation costs in the initial years of an asset's life. This results in a postponement of some tax payments until the later years of an asset's life. Such a postponement of tax liabilities allows firms to make an interest gain by investing the funds which would have been paid as taxes had accelerated depreciation not been allowed. The investment tax credit gives firms a credit against their tax liability of a certain fraction of new investment expenditures on qualifying assets. The major impact of both accelerated depreciation and the investment tax credit has been a reduction in effective corporate tax rates well below the applicable statutory rates. We will not analyze the many details surrounding the impact of accelerated depreciation and investment tax credits on our system of corporate taxation. Instead, throughout the bulk of our discussion, references to "the corporation income tax rate" will mean the effective tax rate taking into account the advantages of accelerated depreciation, the investment tax credit, and other such tax laws.[3]

Finally, we will focus only on the federal corporation income tax and ignore state corporate income taxes. Most states do have some corporation income tax, and those taxes may have a significant effect in our economy. However, a discussion of the effects of such taxes, particularly their effect upon interstate trade and the location of industry, goes well beyond the scope of this study.[4]

---

[2] One of the effects of progressivity of the rate structure has been to encourage large corporations to form multiple corporations to take advantage of the lower tax rate for smaller corporations. This practice has been limited by tax laws, but the incentive remains.

[3] For a discussion of the calculation of such effective tax rates, see Emil M. Sunley, Jr., "Effective Corporate Tax Rates: Toward a More Precise Figure," *Tax Notes*, vol. 4 (March 1, 1976), pp. 15-24.

[4] For a cogent criticism of the use of state corporate income taxes in our economy, see Charles E. McLure, Jr., "State Corporate Income Tax: Lambs in Wolves' Clothing?" U.S. Department of the Treasury, Office of Tax Analysis, no. 25 (March 1977).

1

Why Tax Corporate Profits?

The three most important sources of revenue for the federal government are the personal income tax, the social security payroll tax, and the corporation income tax. Together they account for almost 90 percent of tax revenues. Of these three the corporation income tax raises the smallest amount, and the share of total revenue for which it is responsible has been declining steadily since the Second World War. That decline, however, does not seem to reflect a decision to do away with the tax ultimately or even to reduce it drastically. The principal reason for the decline in the share of federal revenues generated by the corporation income tax has been the rapid increase in the social security program and the consequent rise in payroll taxes. In addition, there has been a decline in the effective rate of corporate taxation, largely because of rules concerning accelerated depreciation and tax credits for investment.[1] In spite of the decline in the *relative* importance of the corporation income tax, revenues from that tax have grown consistently and are currently equal to about 2.6 percent of GNP.

After recognition of the importance of the corporation income tax in the federal tax structure, it remains to ask the reason for this importance. Taxation of personal incomes is a policy firmly grounded in the ability-to-pay approach to taxation—that is, the assumption that taxes should fall most heavily upon those whose ability to pay is greatest because their incomes or their wealth is greatest. Similarly, estate and gift taxes are clearly intended to distinguish among potential taxpayers on the basis of their ability to pay. Social security taxes, on the other hand, are designed primarily as benefit taxes—taxes which fall most heavily upon those who benefit from the expenditure

---

[1] See Emil M. Sunley, Jr., "Effective Corporate Tax Rates," pp. 15-24.

of the tax revenues. In spite of significant disparities between the actual contribution that a person makes and the retirement benefit that he receives, the choice of the payroll as the tax base for financing social security is justified primarily by the benefit principle.

A central issue in the current discussion of the possibility of integrating corporate and personal income taxes is the question of whether the corporation income tax can be rationalized according to the ability-to-pay principle or the benefit principle of taxation. When it was first introduced in 1909 at a rate of 1 percent on income above $5,000, the corporate tax was justified as a benefit tax.[2] In *Flint* v. *Stone Tracey Company*, the Supreme Court characterized the tax as "a tax upon the doing of business with the advantages which inhere in the peculiarities of corporate or joint stock organizations of the character described." However, it is difficult to justify the current tax rate of 46 percent as a charge for benefits. The purpose of a benefit tax is to allocate the costs of some program among those who benefit from the program. While limited liability may provide very large benefits, it is a virtually costless government service.

If the corporation income tax cannot be justified by the benefit principle, can it be justified by the ability-to-pay principle? The response of most economists is that it cannot. The reason for this is simply that, in spite of the legal position of corporations as "persons," they do not possess income. The profits of a corporation are owned by the stockholders and are thus the income of stockholders. This is true even despite the fact that corporate managers may control the disposition of stockholders' income between retentions and dividends. As a result, the tax on corporate profits is a tax on the income of stockholders.[3] This view is often characterized as the conduit view of the corporation.

Viewed as a tax on stockholders' income the corporation income tax clearly cannot be justified by the ability-to-pay principle. The tax

---

[2] Actually there was an earlier corporate tax enacted in 1894 as part of a federal income tax of 2 percent on individual and corporate incomes. That entire act was declared unconstitutional in 1895, however. An even earlier income tax, enacted during the Civil War, did not include a separate tax on corporations, but it did tax stockholders on their shares of corporate profits, whether those profits were distributed or not. In contrast with the 1894 tax, the constitutionality of the Civil War tax was upheld by the Supreme Court in 1870.

[3] This does not reflect a presumption that the ultimate incidence of the tax is on stockholders. For example, Richard Musgrave, a prominent proponent of the view that the corporation income tax is borne by consumers through higher prices, still argues that the tax base is the income of stockholders. See Richard Musgrave and Peggy B. Musgrave, *Public Finance in Theory and Practice* (New York: McGraw-Hill, 1976), chap. 12.

rate is based on the total profits of the corporation, and no attempt is made to provide different tax treatment for stockholders with differing levels of ability to pay.[4] How then can the tax be justified? Richard Goode does so by rejecting the argument that the tax is really a tax on the incomes of stockholders.[5] Stressing the lack of stockholder control over the use of profits, he argues that corporations should be taxed on "their" income as persons.

Stanley S. Surrey also argues that the corporate tax should not be thought of as a tax on stockholders' incomes.[6] He characterizes the conduit view as a bit of "tax theology."[7] Surrey stresses, as Goode does, the control that corporate managers have over the disposition of corporate profits. However, who controls the payout decision or the use of retained earnings is not really relevant to the conduit view. The essential aspect of that view is that, even if managers retain earnings and invest them in projects of their choosing, the stockholders are the ones who gain from the consequent rise in stock values. If the investment projects are not wisely chosen and stock values do not rise by the amount of the earnings retained, then stockholders will have lost some savings. Although the stockholders may not in such instances be able to fire the managers, they can sell their stock and seek firms where their savings—that is, the earnings retained for reinvestment—will not be lost. While such a scenario may be "theology," it does appear to have attracted a number of converts.

---

[4] Of course, it may be that even though the tax *base* is the income of stockholders, the tax does not actually cause any decrease in net corporate profits. Instead, the tax may cause a rise in the prices of corporate products, which may raise the before-tax corporate profits enough to leave net profits unchanged. The burden of the tax is then actually borne by the consumer, who must pay the higher prices. (The possibility of such "shifting" of the tax burden from stockholders to consumers of corporate output and the evidence for it are the subject of Chapter 2.) In this instance the tax is essentially an arbitrary excise tax that still fails to distinguish among the ultimate taxpayers on the basis of their ability to pay. For a more detailed discussion of the corporation income tax and the ability-to-pay and benefit principles of taxation, see Charles E. McLure, Jr., "Integration of the Personal and Corporate Income Taxes: The Missing Element in Recent Tax Reform Proposals," *Harvard Law Review*, vol. 88 (January 1975), pp. 532–82. Peter Mieszkowski discusses the implication of tax shifting for justification of the corporate tax by the ability-to-pay principle in "Integration of the Corporate and Personal Income Taxes: The Bogus Issue of Shifting," *Finanzarchiv*, vol. 31 (1972), pp. 256-97.

[5] Richard Goode, *The Corporation Income Tax* (New York: John Wiley and Sons, 1951).

[6] Stanley S. Surrey, "Reflections on 'Integration' of Corporation and Individual Income Taxes," *National Tax Journal*, vol. 28 (September 1975), pp. 335-40.

[7] Ibid.

The upshot of the foregoing discussion is that a separate tax on corporate profits does not have a sound basis in principles of taxation. Ernest S. Christian reaches a similar conclusion and suggests that "the need for tax revenue is the only reason for the 48 percent non-integrated tax on corporations which exists today."[8] As he realizes, this rationale could justify almost any tax, no matter how odious its effects might be.

The absence of any clear justification for the corporation income tax on either the benefit or the ability-to-pay principle does not mean that there is a consensus among economists that it should be abolished. If it were abolished, a very large amount of current income in the form of retentions would escape taxation or would be taxed only at significantly reduced rates as capital gains. While there are good reasons for taxing capital gains only when they have been realized and then only at reduced rates, these reasons do not apply to retentions. Retentions are a flow of current income that is saved by the corporation for the stockholder. To omit any tax on retentions allows a large loophole for investors to channel their savings through corporations tax-free. The fact that the corporation income tax does impose some tax burden on savings channeled through corporations partially explains why that tax is relied upon so heavily in our revenue system. A more important reason for the popularity of the tax, however, may be that it is a hidden tax—that is, the corporation income tax, unlike the personal income tax or the social security tax, does not include a periodic notice to each taxpayer of the amount of his tax burden. Indeed, most taxpayers probably never know, even approximately, how much their disposable income is reduced by taxes on corporate profits. Consequently, it may be easier for politicians to increase the tax on corporate profits, which is hidden, than to increase taxes on personal income, which are explicit.

It is the fact that abolition of the corporate income tax would allow a great deal of current income to escape full taxation, along with the present double taxation of dividends, which has caused many economists to argue that the appropriate tax policy would be one in which the corporate and personal income taxes were fully integrated. The goal of full integration is to do away with the separate tax treatment of income from corporate sources and to tax all income, no matter what its source, at the personal tax rate of those who have

---

[8] Ernest S. Christian, Jr., "Integrating the Corporate Tax: Methods, Motivations and Effects," research report prepared for Donaldson Lufkin & Jenrette Securities Corporation, New York, and reprinted by the American Enterprise Institute, December 1977, p. 4.

earned that income.[9] More specifically, with full integration dividends would be taxed only once and then at the personal tax rate of the taxpayer who received them. Further, there would be no corporate tax on retained earnings, but those earnings would be allocated to the stockholders—though not actually paid to them—and each stockholder would be liable for personal income taxes on his share of the retentions. The latter adjustment reflects recognition of the fact that retentions are a part of the income of stockholders that is saved by corporations and invested for the benefit of the stockholders.

Short of such a fully integrated income tax system, there have been a number of proposals for partial integration. With a partially integrated system a separate corporate tax on retained earnings would be kept, and there would be no attempt to allocate those retentions to individual stockholders. With such a system the double tax on dividends would be removed, either by allowing corporations to deduct dividends from their taxable profits or by giving stockholders a tax credit for the corporate taxes paid on the dividends they received.[10]

As some form of integration of corporate and personal income taxes has become a more realistic possibility, however, many early proponents of integration have recognized a number of practical administrative problems that might be involved in shifting to a fully integrated—or even a partially integrated—system.[11] Consequently, there appears to be at least a temporary impasse with respect to any broadly based support for tax reform by way of integration. Instead, moderate adjustments in the corporate tax rate itself that do not call

---

[9] For a discussion of the arguments for and against integration, see Charles E. McLure, Jr., "Integration of the Personal and Corporate Income Taxes"; and George F. Break and Joseph A. Pechman, *Federal Tax Reform: The Impossible Dream* (Washington, D.C.: The Brookings Institution, 1975).

[10] See McLure, "Integration of the Corporate and Personal Income Taxes," pp. 550-56, for a more detailed discussion of methods of partial integration.

[11] Treasury Secretary Simon proposed a form of partial integration before the House Ways and Means Committee on July 31, 1975. Full integration is recommended in the U.S. Treasury volume *Blueprints for Basic Tax Reform* (Washington, D.C.: U.S. Government Printing Office, 1977). An interesting example of the growing awareness of the complexities involved in a shift to an integrated tax system is to be found in the writings of McLure. In the current discussion of corporate tax reform he was one of the early advocates of integration. See McLure, "Integration of the Personal and Corporate Income Taxes." However, in his more recent work, he has stressed the uncertainties and difficulties that might arise from integrating the taxes. See Charles E. McLure, Jr., and Stanley S. Surrey, "Integration of Corporation and Individual Income Taxes: Some Issues for Corporate Managers and Other Groups," *Harvard Business Review*, vol. 55 (September-October 1977), pp. 169-81; and Charles E. McLure, Jr., *Must Corporate Income Be Taxed Twice?* (Washington, D.C.: The Brookings Institution, 1979).

for an abrupt change in the tax laws or their administration may well be the practical policy alternative for the near future. Consider, for example, the early discussion by the Carter administration of doing away with the double taxation of dividends and the actual proposal of the administration to reduce the corporate tax rate from 48 percent to 44 percent by 1980. The policy issues that will be dealt with most directly in this study, therefore, are those having to do with the effects of changes in the rate at which the profits of corporations are taxed and not with the likely effects of introducing a system of full or partial integration.

In summary, the corporation income tax is an important part of the federal tax system. In spite of the fact that the imposition of a separate tax on corporate source income has no firm basis in either the ability-to-pay principle or the benefit principle of taxation, it appears that the corporation income tax as a separate tax is likely to remain a significant source of revenue. It is all the more important, therefore, to reach an understanding of the effect of that tax on economic growth, efficiency, and the distribution of income. These are the issues discussed in the following chapters.

2

The Debate over the Short-Run Shifting of the Corporation Income Tax

Ever since the imposition of the U.S. corporation income tax, there has been disagreement as to who actually bears the burden of that tax. The issue is whether corporations can "shift" the tax burden—that is, whether corporations can respond to the imposition of the tax, or to an increase in the tax, in such a way as to prevent their profits after taxes from being reduced. If they are able to do so, the tax burden is not borne by the stockholders but is shifted onto others. In particular, it has been suggested that corporations may be able to raise their prices when the tax is increased, avoiding a reduction in net profits by shifting the tax burden onto the consumers of corporate products.[1] If the tax burden is shifted onto consumers, then the effect of the corporation income tax is similar to that of an excise tax, which exempts—or at least taxes at a lower rate—food and other products the production of which is based largely in the noncorporate sector of the economy. The incidence of such a tax is probably regressive or roughly proportional.[2] On the other hand, since the bulk of privately

---

[1]Another possibility is that corporations may decrease the wages that they offer when the tax is increased, thus shifting the tax burden onto labor. While this possibility is frequently mentioned, it has not attracted much serious consideration in recent literature.

[2] A number of authors treat a shifted corporation income tax as an excise tax on *all* consumption. On the basis of cross-section data showing that the fraction of current income spent on consumption declines as income rises, those authors conclude that the tax is regressive. There are a number of reasons to qualify such conclusions. For example, not all the prices of consumer goods will rise as a result of corporate tax shifting; only the prices of goods produced largely by corporations will rise. Another qualification has to do with the use of data on current annual incomes as opposed to the use of a longer-term income concept, such as lifetime income. There are studies which indicate that consumption as a fraction of lifetime income does not decline very much as income rises. If this is true, the tax may be roughly proportional with respect to lifetime income.

owned stock is held by persons with high incomes, if the tax is not shifted and corporate profits are thereby reduced, the tax will be decidedly progressive.

Whether the tax burden is actually shifted depends upon the adjustments that corporations are able to make and do in fact make when the tax is imposed or increased. Further, what adjustments corporations can make to a tax increase depends on the length of time that has elapsed since the tax increase. In the short run, corporations may be able to adjust their prices, employment, and output, but they will be unable to alter their physical capital stock significantly. In the long run, however, corporations may change their prices, output, and *all* inputs including capital. In Chapter 3 we examine the effect of the corporation income tax in the long run, and there we focus particularly on the capital stock adjustments caused by the tax. In this chapter, however, we investigate the possibility of corporate tax shifting in the short run when firms cannot alter their capital stocks.

Of course, since taxes, once imposed, tend to remain in existence for some time, and the corporation income tax is certainly no exception, it could be argued that the short-run incidence of a tax is not an important issue. However, in the case of the corporation income tax, the long-run incidence and other effects of the tax depend upon the short-run incidence. If the tax is borne by stockholders in the short run, then in the long run the burden may spread to all capitalists or even to all agents in the economy because of a reduction in investment.[3] Further, there may be an inefficient sectoral allocation of capital and a capital shortage may result. On the other hand, if the tax is shifted in the short run, there may be few long-run adjustments, though, as

Recently Edgar Browning has argued that many programs of the federal government for the transfer of income to persons receiving low incomes automatically increase transfer payments in response to increases in the price level. See Edgar K. Browning, "The Burden of Taxation," *Journal of Political Economy,* vol. 86 (August 1978), pp. 649-72. If this is true, the recipients of such transfers would be compensated for any price increases arising from corporate tax shifting, and, thus, such low-income individuals would not bear any of the tax burden. The combined effect of corporate tax shifting and automatic increases in transfers might therefore bring about a progressive distribution.

[3] Notice that such a spreading of the burden does not take place simply upon the sale of a share of stock. This is because, if the tax is not shifted, the short-run burden is capitalized in the form of a decline in stock values. The owners of the stock at the time the tax is imposed suffer a capital loss equal to the capitalized value of the reduction in after-tax profits. Someone who purchased the stock later would bear no short-run burden. The spreading of the burden operates in the long run through changes in physical investment. That process will be discussed in Chapter 3.

will be discussed in the following chapter, a capital shortage may appear even in this case.

The standard method of approaching an issue such as the short-run shifting of the corporation income tax involves specifying a model of the behavior of corporations and other agents in the economy, using that model to obtain specific hypotheses about the extent and nature of any shifting response to tax increases, and finally testing those hypotheses. The method actually used in recent years has followed a chronological sequence just the reverse of standard methodology. In the early and middle 1960s, there was a vigorous debate over econometric tests of shifting that were based on a model with sketchy theoretical underpinnings. Later, more elaborate theoretical models were designed specifically to demonstrate the possibility of the significant tax shifting found in some of the econometric studies. In this chapter the chronological sequence of the debate over short-run shifting will be followed: thus the next section will review some of the recent econometric studies, while the latter two sections will examine theoretical analyses of short-run shifting.

Short-Run Shifting: Econometric Analysis

Does the corporation income tax reduce after-tax profits or do corporations somehow shift the tax burden? At first glance, this question seems to be one that could be fairly easily resolved by a careful analysis of available data. However, a number of detailed econometric studies have failed to resolve this issue. Indeed, the results of the best-known studies tend to indicate extreme estimates of either no shifting of the tax at all or shifting of 100 percent or more. At the same time, on theoretical grounds, there is good reason to believe that annual data on the U.S. manufacturing sector, which are used in many of the empirical studies, should show some, but by no means complete, shifting of the tax. We defer until the following two sections a discussion of the theoretical analysis of this issue. For now, using some examples of recent econometric studies, it is enough to consider the bewildering range of empirical results obtained and the difficulties that must be faced in further studies.

If the effect of the corporation income tax on corporate profits is to be measured, it is necessary to identify all nontax determinants of corporate profits so as to be able to isolate the effect of the tax alone. Further, it is necessary to ensure that the nontax determinants of corporate profits are not themselves influenced by the tax rate. For example, it would be inappropriate to include the price of corporate output as one of the nontax determinants of profits. With the hypothesis of forward tax shifting it is argued that a tax increase would cause firms to raise prices in order to shift the tax. Clearly, to the extent to which they do, the price rise cannot be considered to have caused profits to rise; in fact, the tax caused profits to rise indirectly by raising prices. Including the prices of outputs in a regression equation then would tend to indicate that the tax had less influence on profits than it actually had. In addition, the nontax determinants of corporate profits must be derived from a complete and believable model of the behavior of corporate firms in the U.S. economy. Otherwise, interpretation of the results is open to vast differences of opinion.

In practice, it is virtually impossible to fulfill all these conditions, and empirical research on corporate tax shifting has involved a series of compromises, followed by controversy over the effects of those compromises. For their econometric study of tax shifting, Krzyzaniak and Musgrave chose not to develop an explicit model of the behavior of firms.[4] Instead, by experimentation they chose certain variables that they felt were independent of the corporation income tax rate but that, on purely statistical grounds, were found to be significant determinants of corporate profits. When those variables and the corporate tax rate were used to explain corporate profits in a time-series analysis, Krzyzaniak and Musgrave found more than 100 percent shifting of the tax.[5] That is, their results indicate that an increase in the corporation income tax actually causes after-tax profits to rise.

Richard E. Slitor, Richard Goode, and John G. Cragg, Arnold C. Harberger, and Peter Mieszkowski all disagreed with the results obtained by Krzyzaniak and Musgrave on the ground that a complete model of corporate profits would imply that current macroeconomic conditions are a determinant of those profits.[6] Krzyzaniak and Musgrave's approach implies that corporate profits are not partially determined by the business cycle, that is, their regression equation for corporate profits omits any variable describing current business cycle conditions. As Goode pointed out, the results obtained by Krzyzaniak

---

[4] Marian Krzyzaniak and Richard Musgrave, *The Shifting of the Corporation Income Tax* (Baltimore, Md.: The Johns Hopkins Press, 1963).

[5] Their preferred point estimate indicates shifting of 134 percent.

[6] Richard E. Slitor, "Corporate Tax Incidence: Economic Adjustments to Differentials under a Two-Tier Tax Structure," in *Effects of Corporation Income Tax*, ed. Marian Krzyzaniak (Detroit, Mich.: Wayne State University Press, 1966); Richard Goode, "Rates of Return, Income Shares, and Corporate Tax Incidence," in *Effects of Corporation Income Tax*; John G. Cragg, Arnold C. Harberger, and Peter Mieszkowski, "Empirical Evidence on the Incidence of the Corporation Income Tax," *Journal of Political Economy*, vol. 75 (December 1967), pp. 811-21.

and Musgrave imply that virtually all the recovery in profit rates from the depression years 1936–1939 to the comparatively prosperous years 1955–1957 was attributable to the rise in the corporation income tax rate.[7]

To accept such a conclusion truly strains one's credulity.[8] And yet, it is not clear that inclusion of a business-cycle variable in the estimating equation of Krzyzaniak and Musgrave alters the conclusion that nearly 100 percent of the tax was shifted. Slitor adds to the equation of Krzyzaniak and Musgrave a variable which is the ratio of actual GNP to potential GNP. This reduces the estimate of the amount of the tax that is shifted, but Slitor still finds 87 percent to 96 percent shifting.[9] Cragg, Harberger, and Mieszkowski use the employment rate in the Krzyzaniak and Musgrave regression and find 102 percent shifting. In response to the argument of Krzyzaniak and Musgrave that such business-cycle variables are not independent determinants of corporate profits, but are partially determined by profits and that including such variables causes biased estimates, Cragg, Harberger, and Mieszkowski agree that the business-cycle variables are not truly exogenous; but they point out that the resulting bias causes an over-statement of the degree of shifting.[10] It is not clear, however, how much of an overestimate the 102 percent figure is. It could be significantly reduced and still show a surprisingly large amount of shifting in the short run.

Neither Slitor nor Cragg, Harberger, and Mieszkowski should be interpreted as arguing that the correct estimate of shifting is 86 percent to 102 percent with some upward bias. It was not really the intention of those authors to provide improved estimates of shifting but simply to show that the Krzyzaniak and Musgrave estimating equation, derived as it was from experimentation, is quite sensitive. In this they succeeded; indeed, when Cragg, Harberger, and Mieszkowski included

---

[7] Goode, "Rates of Return," pp. 216-20. As Goode pointed out, the problem is that the movement of tax rates was roughly coincident with that of the business cycle during the period covered by the study by Krzyzaniak and Musgrave.

[8] This is not the only aspect of the results obtained by Krzyzaniak and Musgrave that is difficult to believe. Slitor has shown that their figure of a shifting of 134 percent implies that a rate of return of 6⅔ percent in the absence of a tax will be immediately increased to a *20 percent* before-tax rate of return if a corporate tax of 50 percent is introduced. This result implies an extraordinary degree of restraint on the part of corporations in their quest for profits in the absence of a tax. See Slitor, "Corporate Tax Incidence," p. 166.

[9] Ibid., pp. 158-60.

[10] The Krzyzaniak and Musgrave argument is given in Marian Krzyzaniak and Richard Musgrave, "Discussion," in *Effects of Corporation Income Tax*. See also, Cragg, Harberger, and Mieszkowski, "Empirical Evidence," pp. 814-17.

a dummy variable for the war mobilization years, they found no significant evidence of shifting at all.[11] Ultimately, the basic issue in the debate over the results obtained by Krzyzaniak and Musgrave is not the omission of a business-cycle variable but the lack of an explicit theoretical model to justify their estimating equation. In responding to Cragg, Harberger, and Mieszkowski, Krzyzaniak and Musgrave themselves agreed that the shifting question remains open until there is some econometric work explicitly based on a complete theoretical model.[12]

Recently, there have been a number of attempts to estimate the extent of shifting on the basis of detailed models of the determination of profits. Unfortunately, the results of those studies have not narrowed the range of shifting estimates. Among others, Robert Gordon, Joan Turek, and William H. Oakland found little or no shifting.[13] In each of these studies a different approach was taken: Gordon hypothesized markup pricing; Turek left pricing policies somewhat loosely specified but followed a factor-shares production function approach; and Oakland explicitly assumed profit-maximizing pricing policies.[14] A significant point raised in these papers is the importance of taking into account the increased productivity of capital during the sample period. Gordon and Oakland, in particular, stress that failure to take into account the increased productivity of capital and the much-discussed omission of a business-cycle variable may have been the principal reasons for the high estimates of shifting obtained by Krzyzaniak and Musgrave.

---

[11] Cragg, Harberger, and Mieszkowski, "Empirical Evidence," pp. 817–18. Krzyzaniak and Musgrave respond to this by arguing that a better procedure is to omit those years or estimate separate coefficients of shifting for peacetime and periods of mobilization for war. Both these procedures result in estimates of shifting of more than 100 percent. But this sensitivity to the way in which the war years are treated really only points up the general sensitivity of results alleged by the critics of the Krzyzaniak and Musgrave study. See Marian Krzyzaniak and Richard Musgrave, "Corporate Tax Shifting: A Response," *Journal of Political Economy*, vol. 78 (July/August 1970), pp. 768-73. See also, John Cragg, Arnold Harberger, and Peter Mieszkowski, "Rejoinder," *Journal of Political Economy*, vol. 78 (July/August 1970), pp. 774-77.

[12] Krzyzaniak and Musgrave, "A Response," p. 770.

[13] Robert Gordon, "Incidence of a Corporation Income Tax," *American Economic Review*, vol. 57 (September 1967), pp. 731-58; Joan Turek, "Short-Run Shifting of a Corporation Income Tax in Manufacturing, 1935-1965," *Yale Economic Essays*, vol. 10 (Spring 1970), pp. 127-48; William H. Oakland, "Corporate Earnings and Tax Shifting in U.S. Manufacturing, 1930-1968," *Review of Economics and Statistics*, vol. 54 (August 1972), pp. 235-44.

[14] Turek's approach is a generalization of that followed by Challis Hall, Jr., "Direct Shifting of the Corporation Income Tax in Manufacturing," *American Economic Review*, vol. 54 (May 1964), pp. 258-71.

However, Richard Dusansky examined tax shifting in a study in which he allowed for increases in the productivity of capital and business-cycle conditions, and yet he found shifting of more than 100 percent.[15] It is particularly disconcerting to anyone following the econometric analysis of short-run shifting of the corporation income tax to note that the studies of Dusansky and Oakland, in spite of their widely differing conclusions, are fairly similar. In both studies the rate of return on capital for U.S. manufacturing firms was regressed on the labor–capital ratio, the effective tax rate, a variable intended to measure changes in technology, and a business-cycle variable.[16] Oakland also included a lagged business-cycle variable, while Dusansky included the ratio of inventory to sales, the ratio of employee compensation to the aggregate price level, and the ratio of a materials price level to the aggregate price level.[17] Oakland found the tax variable to be totally insignificant, while the business-cycle variable, the labor–capital ratio, and the technological-change variable were all highly significant and explained 91 percent of the variation in rates of profit. Dusansky, on the other hand, found his business-cycle variable and technological-change variable to be quite insignificant. He found that 91 percent of the variation in profit rates could be explained by the ratio of inventory to sales, the ratio of the price of materials to total prices, the labor–capital ratio, and, most significant of all, the tax rate. His best estimate indicates 102 percent short-run shifting.

Objections can be raised to almost any empirical study, and the studies by Goode, Turek, Oakland, and Dusansky are not exceptions.[18] Oakland, for example, explicitly designed his model under the assumption of the maximization of profits, which is inconsistent with shifting.

---

[15] Richard Dusansky, "The Short-Run Shifting of the Corporation Income Tax in the United States," *Oxford Economic Papers*, vol. 24 (November 1972), pp. 357-71.

[16] Of course, these variables were not measured in the same way by Oakland and Dusansky. However, there does not seem to be any compelling reason to say that one choice of measurement is clearly superior. For example, the business-cycle variable used by Oakland is the unemployment rate in manufacturing, while that used by Dusansky is the ratio of actual GNP to potential GNP. Such differences do not provide a firm basis for completely rejecting one study or the other.

[17] This refers to Oakland's equations 3, 5, and 7, and to Dusansky's equation 1.1.

[18] Krzyzaniak and Musgrave offered several objections to Goode's analysis. See Marian Krzyzaniak and Richard Musgrave, "Incidence of the Corporation Income Tax in U.S. Manufacturing: Comment," *American Economic Review*, vol. 58 (December 1968), pp. 1358-60; and Robert Gordon, "Incidence of the Corporation Income Tax in U.S. Manufacturing: Reply," *American Economic Review*, vol. 58 (December 1968), pp. 1360-67.

He interpreted the insignificance of a tax term which had been added to that model as implying that no shifting had occurred. A more complete test would involve constructing a model on the assumption that profits would not be maximized, testing the extent of shifting in that context, and comparing the overall accuracy of that model with the profit-maximizing model.

Dusansky did attempt to formulate an estimating equation which was at least loosely based on goals other than maximizing profits. He alluded specifically to sales and inventory goals in addition to a profit goal. Among other possible objections, however, is the argument that his choice of exogenous variables was suspect and was even inconsistent with the models he referred to in which profits were not maximized. For example, he assumed that expenditures for advertising are exogenous to the tax rate, and yet, as is discussed more fully below, short-run shifting by firms that try to maximize sales or a function of sales and profits implies that expenditures for advertising fall and prices of outputs rise when the tax is increased. The adjustment in advertising expenditure is an integral part of the shifting process, and the advertising variable should not be taken a priori as exogenous.

But resolving objections such as these is unlikely to achieve a final consensus on the short-run shifting of the corporation income tax. Instead, it is necessary to disaggregate data concerning the manufacturing sector and look at the behavior of separate industries. Most theoretical models of tax shifting make it clear that a necessary, but not sufficient, condition for tax shifting is the existence of market power. Since in 1970 fully 20 percent of the value of manufacturing output was produced by industries in which the largest four firms produce less than 20 percent of industry output, one must look with considerable skepticism at any study, no matter how sophisticated the econometric tests used, in which it is suggested that 100 percent or more of the corporation income tax was shifted for the entire U.S. manufacturing sector.

On the other hand, if what shifting does occur comes from the more concentrated industries in the manufacturing sector, then a study of that entire sector in which tax shifting is found to be statistically insignificant cannot be relied upon for the conclusion that shifting does not occur or even that it is not fairly widespread. Statistical insignificance of shifting could arise from "noise" in the aggregate data stemming from changing shares in aggregate profits of those industries in which shifting occurs or from changes in profit rates in those industries caused by exogenous industry-specific factors. In this regard, it is interesting to note that Gordon, Turek, and Oakland find point estimates of shifting which range from around 2 percent up to 34 percent, all of which are, however, highly insignificant statistically. That is, in the studies which are often used to support the zero-shifting hypothesis, precise estimates of very small shifting are not attained; instead, quite imprecise estimates of an economically significant level of shifting are found in some instances—those that contain estimates of shifting of more than 20 percent.

There have been some disaggregate studies of tax shifting. Interestingly enough, one of them is Gordon's study in which insignificant shifting in the aggregate is found.[19] From his results for ten separate industries, it is clear that his conclusion in the aggregate case stems from widely varying results at the industry level. For the two most concentrated industries, Gordon obtains highly significant estimates of around 90 percent shifting. For the fourth most concentrated industry, the estimate is a highly significant 44 percent. For the least concentrated industries the estimates of shifting are generally small and insignificant.[20]

In a review of Gordon's work, E. Cary Brown stressed the importance of the disaggregated estimates of shifting.[21] Making some plausible adjustments in Gordon's industry results, Brown aggregated those results and achieved an estimate of 24 percent shifting by the entire manufacturing sector.[22] Not only is this method of calculating aggregate shifting more reasonable than that used in the econometric

[19] Gordon's disaggregate analysis is open to the objections raised by Krzyzaniak and Musgrave in their comment on his article. Gordon's defense also applies. See Krzyzaniak and Musgrave, "Comment," pp. 1358-60, and Gordon, "Reply," pp. 1360-67. In their comment Krzyzaniak and Musgrave never mentioned Gordon's disaggregate results. It is unfortunate that most attention has been drawn to Gordon's aggregate results; his results for various industries are interesting and indicate a need for further disaggregate research.

[20] Gordon found negative shifting in a number of instances, three of which are statistically significant. Because the theoretical rationale for negative shifting is extremely weak, however, those results must be viewed with some skepticism. Since the aggregate results are influenced by such potentially spurious results for the industry, his aggregate conclusions must also be viewed cautiously.

[21] E. Cary Brown, "Recent Studies of the Incidence of the Corporation Income Tax," in Public Finance and Stabilization Policy: Essays in Honor of Richard A. Musgrave, ed. Warren L. Smith and John M. Culbertson (Amsterdam: North-Holland Publishing Co., 1974), pp. 93-108.

[22] Brown treated the statistically significant estimates of negative shifting as showing zero shifting. Since there is almost no theoretical basis for expecting negative shifting, this is a reasonable adjustment. He also treated all shifting estimates which are positive but statistically insignificant at the 5 percent level as estimates of zero shifting. This is not appropriate since, even if the estimate is insignificantly different from zero, it is still a statistical estimate of the degree of shifting that is preferable to zero. Using the proper estimates, however, does not have much effect on Brown's results.

studies that are based directly on aggregate data, but Brown's estimate is also more plausible than the zero or 100 percent extremes. More careful disaggregated estimates of shifting are needed, however, before any consensus can be reached.

One of the industries in which shifting behavior might be expected is the privately owned electric utilities industry. Because of regulation or the threat of regulation, such firms may not maximize profits. Thus, they may be able to raise before-tax profits when the tax is increased.[23] John L. Mikesell used an approach very similar to Oakland's to study tax shifting in privately owned electric utilities.[24] He found shifting of almost 58 percent. This finding is interesting not only because of the disaggregate nature of the study, but also because he obtained a more believable estimate of middle-range shifting.[25]

An overview of these econometric analyses of short-run shifting indicates that most of the sound and the fury over this issue has dealt with aggregate studies of the U.S. manufacturing sector. In the end, however, the results of such studies may signify little or nothing. Since the manufacturing sector is made up of many industries in which firms operate under distinctly different conditions of competition, it might be expected that to identify accurately any shifting behavior with respect to that entire sector would be difficult. Viewed in this light, the extreme sensitivity of the aggregate studies, which is the salient feature of that literature, is not surprising. A promising avenue for future research, already initiated in a few instances, is an examination of patterns of shifting by particular industries. Only by working at an industry level and then aggregating the results can an accurate measure of economywide shifting of the corporation income tax in the short run be obtained.

---

[23] More specifically, they may be able to persuade regulators to allow a price increase when the tax is raised.

[24] John L. Mikesell, "The Corporation Income Tax and the Rate of Return in Privately-Owned Electric Utilities," *Public Finance*, vol. 28 (1973), pp. 291-300.

[25] One other study must be mentioned. William R. Moffat examined the short-run effect of the corporation income tax on prices in the textile industries. Though he did not attempt to measure shifting, his results are of interest here. Since the textile industry is moderately competitive, it might be expected that little shifting would occur. Moffat found that the tax had a very small but statistically significant positive effect on prices. This is one instance in which the hypothesis of a small tax effect is corroborated by a small but statistically significant coefficient. Moffat also looked at price data in the rubber industries, but his results in that part of his study were ambiguous. See William R. Moffat, "Taxes in the Price Equation: Textiles and Rubber," *Review of Economics and Statistics*, vol. 52 (August 1970), pp. 253-61.

Theoretical Analysis of the Short-Run Incidence of the Corporation Income Tax: Traditional Theories of Firm Behavior

If a firm maximizes its pure profits, then, with one exception, noted below, a tax on those pure profits will cause after-tax profits to fall by the amount of the tax and will leave all prices and outputs unchanged. This conclusion is commonly offered as an argument that if firms maximize profits, the corporation income tax is borne by stockholders. For that purpose, however, the argument is not quite complete. The corporation income tax is assessed against the total profits earned by a corporation, not just its pure profits. The total profits earned by a firm are the sum of its pure profits and its normal profits. The distinction between normal profits and pure profits is quite important to an analysis of taxes on profits. Normal profits are the return that firms must offer investors in order to attract and retain investment funds. Normal profits are a cost of doing business in the same sense that wages that must be paid to attract laborers are a cost. Simply put, wages are the cost to a firm of labor, and normal profits are the cost of capital. In the economy as a whole, normal profits are determined by the productivity of capital. Pure profits, sometimes called economic, or excess profits, are the difference between total revenues and total costs, including the cost of capital— that is, normal profits. Profit-maximizing firms seek to maximize pure profits, not total (pure plus normal) profits.

With this clarification, the argument given above can be completed and used to describe the effect of a tax on the total profits earned by a firm.[26] If in the absence of a tax the firm maximizes its

---

[26] Actually, not all normal profits are subject to the corporation income tax. The normal profits of that portion of the firm's capital stock which is financed by debt are the interest payments on that debt. The U.S. tax laws explicitly recognize interest payments as a cost to the firm and allow them to be deducted from the tax base. The discussion here of normal profits really only points out that equity finance, just like debt finance, involves a cost that must be paid to investors in order to attract and keep investment funds. With respect to debt finance that cost is interest payments; with respect to equity finance it is a fair return in the form of dividends and capital gains.

In order to simplify the discussion, we will assume throughout this chapter and the next, that firms do not alter the proportion of their capital which is debt-financed in response to changes in the tax rate. This will allow us to take the effective tax rate on capital as exogenous to the firm. For example, suppose that 80 percent of the capital stock of a firm is equity-financed and the corporation income tax rate is 50 percent. These figures imply an effective tax on normal profits of 40 percent—50 percent of 80 percent. In Chapter 4 we examine recent analysis which takes into account the fact that firms may raise the proportion of their capital stock which is debt-financed so as to lower, or even completely avoid, the corporate tax on normal profits.

pure profits, then the firm will be unable to raise those profits to a higher level after a tax has been imposed, so pure profits after tax must decline by the amount of the tax on pure profits. Further, in the short run when each firm's capital stock is fixed, the normal return earned by capital is also fixed, and capital is said to be earning a quasi-rent. Thus normal profits after tax must decline by the amount of the tax on normal profits. This completes the argument: if firms maximize profits, then the corporation income tax assessed against total profits— pure profits plus normal profits—is borne by stockholders. Notice that the reasoning does not depend upon whether the firms are perfect competitors or whether they have monopoly power. As long as firms seek to maximize pure profits, the tax is borne in the short run by stockholders.[27]

While this argument is fairly commonly accepted, some qualification is necessary. Martin S. Feldstein pointed out that such conclusions may be altered if the portfolio choices of investors are taken into account.[28] The argument of the preceding paragraph implies that imposition of a corporation income tax will, in the short run, reduce stock prices by the capitalized value of the taxes. This capital loss represents the burden on current owners of the firm. The rate of return on the reduced value of the stock and the risk associated with that return— measuring risk as the standard deviation of the return in relation to the price of the stock—would not change. Consequently, if the portfolios of investors were in equilibrium before the imposition of the tax, then once the tax had been imposed and stock prices had declined, investors would find that portion of the value of their portfolios which was in corporate equity to be too low. By increasing their stock holdings and reducing their holdings of other assets, investors will bid the price of stocks up in relation to the prices of other assets. As a result of this rise in stock prices, the overall decline in stock prices

---

[27] This argument is based on a strict interpretation of the short run as the period in which all capital is in fixed supply. The econometric studies discussed in the preceding section take the short run to be one year. As Brown pointed out some time ago, the corporation income tax falls on working capital invested in variable assets such as inventories. Even in the instance of a profit-maximizing firm, a tax on such variable costs may be partially shifted in a year's time and thus will appear as short-run shifting in econometric studies. The process by which shifting of a tax on variable costs occurs is taken up in detail in the next chapter, in the discussion of long-run tax incidence. E. Cary Brown, "The Corporate Tax in the Short Run," *National Tax Journal*, vol. 7 (September 1954), pp. 240-41.

[28] Martin S. Feldstein, "The Surprising Incidence of a Tax on Pure Rent: A New Answer to an Old Question," *Journal of Political Economy*, vol. 85 (April 1977), pp. 349-60.

that is attributable to the tax is less than the capitalized value of the tax receipts. Accordingly, investors, in their capacities as stockholders, do not bear all the tax even in the short run.[29]

While taking into account the qualifications pointed out by Feldstein, it is probably safe to conclude that if firms are profit maximizers, most of the short-run burden of the corporation income tax is borne by stockholders. Any short-run shifting that occurs because of the adjustments in portfolios discussed by Feldstein will cause the same stockholders to bear some of the burden in their capacity as holders of noncorporate assets and will cause some investors who do not own any stock, but who hold other assets, to bear a burden. This redistributes some of the burden among capitalists but does not induce significant shifting of the tax onto consumers.

In addition to the points raised by Feldstein, the simple argument at the beginning of this section must be qualified if uncertainty is taken into account. Rudolph G. Penner stayed within the traditional approach to the behavior of firms—as opposed to the approaches discussed in the following section—but, because he assumed uncertainty with respect to the price of output, he found that stockholders may bear more or less than 100 percent of the tax burden in the short run.[30] If the management of the firm is risk-neutral, then the firm will maximize expected profits and stockholders will bear exactly 100 percent of the tax. If, however, management is risk-averse, then the firm will choose a lower level of output and a higher price than that which maximizes expected profits. To see why this is so, note that at the output at which expected profit is maximized, marginal cost is equal to expected marginal revenue. But the risk-averse firm essentially discounts marginal revenue because of the uncertainty concerning actual prices. Accordingly, the risk-averse firm chooses a level of output at which marginal cost is equal to expected marginal revenue minus the discount that is attributable to uncertainty. Since at this level of output marginal cost is less than expected marginal revenue, output is lower and price is higher than at the expected profit maximum.

A tax on the firm's pure profits will not alter the marginal cost or expected marginal revenue schedules; its only direct effect on the

---

[29] Even this conclusion must be qualified. The investors who actually shift their portfolios by purchasing more equity do not benefit from the rise in stock prices, for they must pay those higher prices. But stockholders who do not change their portfolios will benefit from the rise in stock prices.

[30] Rudolph G. Penner, "Uncertainty and the Short-Run Shifting of the Corporation Tax," *Oxford Economic Papers*, vol. 19 (March 1967), pp. 95-110.

firm's choice of output and price arises from the effect of the tax on the uncertainty discount applied to expected marginal revenues.[31] If the uncertainty discount is reduced, then the gap between expected marginal revenue and marginal cost must be reduced; thus the firm will expand output and reduce price, moving closer to the profit maximum. This causes before-tax profits to rise so that net profits fall by an amount that is less than the tax revenues.[32] If, on the other hand, the uncertainty discount rises, the gap between marginal cost and expected marginal revenue increases, causing the firm to move away from the profit maximum by raising prices and reducing revenues. In this instance, after-tax profits fall by an amount that is greater than the tax revenues.

There are two factors that cause the uncertainty discount to change when a tax is introduced. The first is a result of the fact that, since the tax causes the government to share in the profits, the government also shares the risk. This sharing of the risk with the government causes the uncertainty discount to decline. The effect of the second factor on the discount depends upon whether or not the risk-aversion of managers rises or falls as profits rise. If managers' risk-aversion rises as profits rise—that is, if they display increasing absolute risk-aversion—then the *decline* in profits induced by the tax causes a decline in the uncertainty discount, reinforcing the decline resulting from sharing the risk with the government. In this instance, the firm will reduce price and expand output, and stockholders will bear less than 100 percent of the tax.

If, on the other hand, managers display decreasing absolute risk-aversion, then the tax-induced decline in profits increases risk-aversion and thus increases the uncertainty discount. This works in the opposite direction from the effect of sharing the risk with the government and may, if risk-aversion responds sharply to the fall in profits, cause the overall effect to be an increase in the uncertainty discount. If that occurs, prices rise, output declines, and stockholders bear more than 100 percent of the tax.

While Penner's analysis indicates that some short-run tax shifting can occur even in the context of the traditional theory of the firm, it

---

[31] If the firm is risk-neutral, there is no uncertainty discount and the tax will have no effect on output or price. This is what generates the result, mentioned above, that stockholders of a risk-neutral firm bear 100 percent of the tax burden in the short run.

[32] Normally when after-tax profits rise and, thus, net profits do not fall by the amount of the tax revenues, the tax is said to have been shifted. In this instance, however, wages do not change and prices actually fall. As a result, though the tax can be said to have been shifted, it is not at all clear to whom the tax burden has been shifted.

does not provide—nor was it intended to provide—a rationale for the significant degree of tax-shifting throughout the corporate sector found in some econometric studies. This is true for a number of reasons. As Penner pointed out, because of the diversity of firms and their responses to risk, it is unlikely that any aggregate shifting response comparable to the shifting he examined at the level of an individual firm could be isolated clearly in an empirical study of tax shifting. Further, the case in which net profits can be expected to decline the least is the one in which risk-aversion increases as profits rise, since in that case the change in risk-aversion and the sharing of risk with the government both act to keep profits from declining very much. However, it is usually agreed that individuals are likely to exhibit decreasing absolute risk-aversion, not increasing risk-aversion—the point being that a person whose income is low is likely to be less willing to accept a given risk than is a very rich person. Finally, increasing absolute risk-aversion cannot be combined with the risk-sharing effect to bring about shifting of 100 percent or more. If the tax is shifted 100 percent, then net profits do not change, so whether risk-aversion rises or falls with profits is irrelevant. Consequently, the only factor in Penner's model that could induce the 100 percent shifting observed in some econometric studies is the effect of sharing the risk with the government. This does not, of course, mean that shifting of 100 percent is impossible in the model, but it does indicate that it is unlikely.[33]

Theoretical Analysis of Short-Run Shifting: Non–Profit-Maximizing Models

If little or no shifting of the tax in the short run is predicted in traditional models of profit-maximizing behavior, then a rationalization of the econometric findings of significant short-run shifting must be based on non–profit-maximizing firm behavior. There have been a number of models involving some form of non–profit-maximizing managerial decision making which have been used to demonstrate the possibility of significant short-run shifting. In virtually all these studies either it has been assumed explicitly that the corporation income tax does not reduce the normal return to capital, thus begging much of the question, or the tax has been treated as simply a tax on pure profits, thus ignoring much of the issue.

---

[33] Penner did not address the issue of the degree of tax shifting but only the direction of change in output, prices, and profits induced by a tax on profits.

One of the best known of these models is William J. Baumol's model of sales maximization subject to a constraint on minimum acceptable profits.[34] In that model, the minimum profit constraint is essentially the normal return to capital—that is, it is the amount that the firm must earn for its investors in order to be able to attract and hold their investments.[35] Levy used Baumol's model to examine the incidence of the corporation income tax.[36] Since Levy's analysis and his conclusion that the tax is fully shifted are repeated rather widely, we will sketch his reasoning here.

In Figure 1 quantity sold is measured along the horizontal axis. The curve labeled R represents total revenues; the curve labeled C represents total costs, except the cost of capital—that is, the normal return to capital; and the curve labeled π is given by $R-C$ and is thus total profits—that is, pure profits plus normal profits. The horizontal line labeled π_c is the minimum-profit constraint—that is, it represents the normal return to capital.[37] Revenues are maximized at an output level of Q_1 where the firm earns zero pure profits. If a tax, t, is now imposed on the total profits of the firm and *if the tax does not reduce the normal return to capital*, then the firm's profit constraint rises to $\pi_c/(1-t)$, the sales-maximizing level of output declines to Q_t, and the tax is shifted forward in the form of higher prices.[38]

Clearly, if the intention is to examine the effect of the corporation income tax on the total return to capital, the use of Baumol's model by Levy and many subsequent authors begs much of the question.

[34] William J. Baumol, *Business Behavior, Value and Growth*, rev. ed. (New York: Harcourt Brace and World, 1967).

[35] Ibid., p. 50.

[36] Michael E. Levy, "Professor Baumol's Oligopolistic Model and the Corporation Income Tax," *Public Finance*, vol. 16 (1961), pp. 366-72.

[37] In most discussions of this model it is not pointed out that the C curve does not include the cost of capital. However, if the profit constraint measures the normal return to capital as Baumol indicates, then the cost of capital could not be included in C. If it were included, then at Q_1, where total profits are just equal to normal profits, a C curve including the cost of capital would intersect the R curve.

[38] Actually, part—or conceivably all—of the reductions in revenues could be the result of a reduction in advertising expenditures with no increase in price. An important aspect of Baumol's model, which is not usually mentioned when that model is applied to the issue of tax shifting, is that firms increase revenues both by reducing prices and by raising advertising expenditures and decrease revenues both by raising prices and by reducing advertising expenditures (see Baumol, *Business Behavior*, pp. 58-60). Without this assumption, the profit constraint may not be binding, in which case, even with the assumption that the normal rate of return to capital is unaffected by the tax, pure profits will decline when a tax is imposed and there is little or no tax shifting.

FIGURE 1

The Effect of a Tax on the Profits of a Revenue-Maximizing Firm

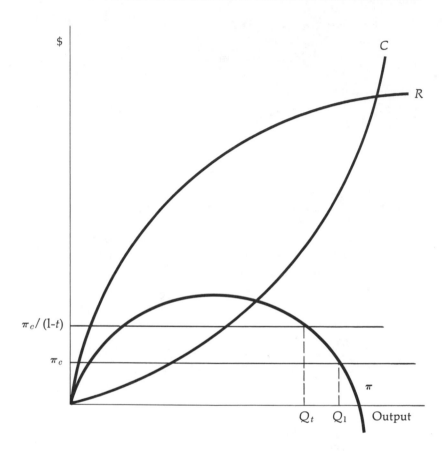

It is simply and directly assumed that the tax does not cause any reduction in the normal return to capital. If the tax in question were assessed only against a few sales-maximizing firms, such an assumption might be justified fairly easily. But the U.S. corporation income tax is assessed against a very large number of firms which produce the bulk of total U.S. output and which are certainly not all sales maximizers. An assumption that the tax leaves the normal rate of return unchanged, therefore, requires considerable justification. Indeed, that issue is the crux of the problem.

There have been a number of studies in which tax incidence has been examined by the use of a generalized version of Baumol's model or versions of the managerial-discretion models developed by Oliver E. Williamson.[39] While the effect of the tax on the normal return to capital was ignored in these studies and they are thus subject to the objection made above, they do offer some interesting implications. For example, suppose that managers maximize a utility function the arguments of which are pure profits and total revenues.[40] In Figure 2, the curve OAZ shows possible combinations of pure profits and revenues that the firm can expect when there is no tax. II is an indifference curve based on the managerial utility function $U = U(\pi,R)$. (Note that now π represents only *pure* profits.)

While the profit-maximizing firm will choose point A, the firm that maximizes $U(\pi,R)$ will seek more revenues than at A and thus choose a point such as B, where it earns π_1 in pure profits and has R_1 in total revenues. If a tax on pure profits alone is imposed, then the after-tax pure profits obtained at various levels of revenue will lie below OAZ. Suppose that when a tax is imposed, net profits are given by the curve OCZ, and the firm chooses a point to the left of E—that is to say, the firm responds to the tax by raising prices and reducing revenues, thereby causing gross profits to rise above their level at B. As a result, much of the tax is shifted. In general, however, the tax may not be shifted; indeed, net profits may decline by an amount greater than the amount of the tax revenues. This occurs if the firm chooses a point to the right of E on OCZ.

What point the firm chooses on OCZ, and thus whether or not shifting occurs, depends upon two effects that are analogous to the income and substitution effects of demand analysis. The two effects

---

[39] See, for example, Oliver E. Williamson, *The Economics of Discretionary Behavior: Managerial Objectives in a Theory of the Firm* (Chicago: Markham Publishing Company, 1967), appendix 4a, pp. 61-65; A. A. Bayer, "Shifting of the Corporation Income Tax and Various Theories of Firm Behavior," *Public Finance*, vol. 25 (1970), pp. 449-61; F. D. Sebold, "Short-Run Tax Response in a Utility-Maximizing Framework," *National Tax Journal*, vol. 23 (1970), pp. 365-72; and John Cauley and Tod Sandler, "The Short-Run Shifting of the Corporation Income Tax: A Theoretical Investigation," *Public Finance*, vol. 29 (1974), pp. 19-35.

[40] This is a simplified example of the utility function used in the studies mentioned in note 39. Those studies also include variables such as expenditures for staff and administration, managerial emoluments, and output in the utility function. In most of them the profit variable is not identified as pure profits, though Williamson, in *Economics of Discretionary Behavior*, does indicate that it is profit in excess of a minimum profit demanded by stockholders. For the model to be sufficiently realistic to be useful, it is clear that the profit variable in the utility function cannot include normal profits—that is, managers may be able and willing to reduce pure profits in order to obtain greater revenues, but, since normal profits are the cost of acquiring and keeping capital, normal profits cannot be reduced to obtain additional revenues.

FIGURE 2

THE EQUILIBRIUM OF A UTILITY-MAXIMIZING FIRM

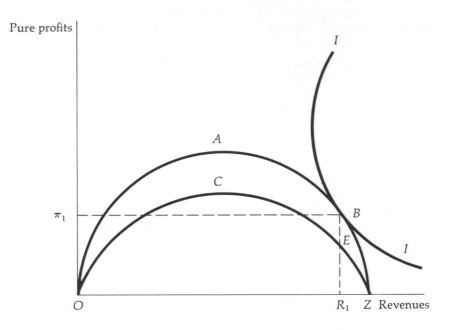

arise because imposing such a tax not only reduces net profits for each level of revenue but also reduces the cost of extra revenue in terms of forgone profits. To understand those two effects, suppose that a tax of 50 percent is imposed on profits and that the firm moves initially from point B to point E, which is to say that initially the tax causes profits to be cut in half while revenues are left unchanged. It seems plausible to expect the utility-maximizing firm to recoup some of the profit that has been lost by reducing revenues, moving to the left of E. This is one effect of the tax, and it leads to shifting. The second effect, however, tends to mitigate or reverse any shifting. Turning to the second effect and continuing with the numerical example, suppose that at point B five dollars in additional revenue costs the firm one dollar in forgone profits—that is, the slope of OAZ at B is -5. Since in the absence of the tax, B is the point at which utility is maximized, we know that at B management is just indifferent to the possibility of obtaining five dollars in additional revenues at the cost of one dollar in the forgone profits; this means that the slope of the indifference curve at B is -5 also. When the tax is imposed and the firm moves initially to point E, five dollars in additional revenues costs the firm only fifty cents in forgone after-tax profits.[41] Clearly, the cost of additional revenues in terms of net profits forgone has fallen, thereby inducing a tendency for the firm to increase revenues—by lowering prices—and reduce profits—that is, inducing the firm to move to the right of E. Which of the two effects will dominate and whether or not there will be any shifting cannot be determined in advance. The final result depends on the particular form of the utility function—or even its existence—as well as the precise shape of the revenue-profit curve OAZ. Both of these, but particularly the former, are extremely difficult to determine empirically.

Thus, the usefulness of these models for incidence analysis is limited. They do describe a pattern of behavior that might lead to short-run shifting of a tax on pure profits. That same pattern of behavior, however, might cause the full burden of the tax—or even more than the full burden—to be borne by profits. Further, as has been stressed repeatedly, little or nothing can be learned from these models about the burden of a tax that falls on normal profits as well as on pure profits.

The latter point applies not only to the managerial-discretion models mentioned above, but also to other models of non–profit-maximizing behavior that are used in the attempt to demonstrate the possibility of short-run shifting of the corporation income tax. It has been argued that if oligopolists set prices so as to keep rivals from entering their industry, shifting of 100 percent of the tax may occur.[42] As stressed by George Break, however, this result "is based on the highly restrictive assumption that normal profit rates are not lowered by the tax."[43] A similar analysis of the behavior of oligopolists by David M. Reaume has the same shortcoming;[44] so does the often vaguely specified argument that firms set prices by adding a markup to costs exclusive of the cost of capital. (We are still ignoring debt and

---

[41] At point E, five dollars in extra revenue still reduces before-tax profits by one dollar, but because of the 50 percent tax, this only reduces after-tax profits by fifty cents. In general, the slope of OCZ for any value of R is $(1-t)$ times the slope of OAZ at the same value of R. Since the slope of OCZ shows the cost of extra revenues in forgone profits, when t rises, that cost falls.

[42] See, for example, Sergio Bruno, "Corporation Income Tax, Oligopolistic Markets, and Immediate Tax Shifting: A Suggested Theoretical Approach," *Public Finance*, vol. 25 (1970), pp. 363-78.

[43] George Break, "The Incidence and Economic Effects of Taxation," in *The Economics of Public Finance* (Washington, D.C.: The Brookings Institution, 1974), p. 142, note 44.

[44] David M. Reaume, "Short-Run Corporate Tax Shifting by Profit-Maximizing Oligopolists," *Public Finance Quarterly*, vol. 4 (January 1976), pp. 33-44.

interest payments, so capital costs are the normal returns to stock-holders.) It seems unlikely that the size of the markup chosen by a firm will be completely independent of rates of return earned else-where—that is, it will not be independent of the normal rate of return. Consequently, the assumption that the markup is unchanged when a corporation income tax is imposed is a veiled form of the assumption that the normal return to capital is unaffected by the tax.

J. Gregory Ballentine uses a simple model of non–profit-maximizing, managerial-discretionary behavior in which he deals explicitly with a tax that falls on both pure profits and normal profits.[45] He assumes that the utility of managers is a function of pure profits and total revenues or total output. Conceptually, the tax on corporate profits examined in that model can be separated into two taxes, a tax on pure profits and a tax on normal profits. The tax on pure profits has the same effect as the tax discussed above by means of Figure 2. It may be fully shifted forward through price increases or it may not. The tax on normal profits has a much more certain effect. In the long run, capital is mobile throughout the economy, and the normal return to capital that a firm must pay is determined by the rate of return, after tax, that investors can receive from other firms. In the short run, each firm's capital stock is fixed and the normal return to capital before tax is a quasi-rent. A tax on capital earning a quasi-rent is borne entirely by capitalists.[46] As a result, in the model used by Ballentine, the short-run incidence of the corporation income tax depends upon two things: the extent to which the tax on pure profits is shifted and the share of normal profits in total profits. If most of total profits are simply the normal return to capital, then capitalists will bear the bulk of the burden of the corporation income tax no matter how much of the tax on pure profits is shifted.

Whether such a conclusion is accepted or not, theoretical analyses in which the attempt is made to rationalize the econometric evidence indicating significant short-run tax shifting must deal with a tax that falls on the total profits of the firm and must not assume that the

[45] J. Gregory Ballentine, "Non-Profit Maximizing Behavior and the Short-Run Incidence of the Corporation Income Tax," *Journal of Public Economics*, vol. 7 (1977), pp. 135-46. The model used there is a simple general-equilibrium model including both corporate and noncorporate firms. Noncorporate firms are assumed to maximize their profits. The full general-equilibrium adjustments to the corporation income tax in that model imply only slight modifications of the results discussed in the text. In the long run, when firms can increase or decrease their capital stock, the general equilibrium adjustments become much more impor-tant. The long-run effects of the tax will be taken up in the next chapter.
[46] In arriving at this conclusion the qualifications raised by Feldstein in "The Surprising Incidence," which were discussed above, were ignored.

normal rate of return is unaffected by the tax. Except for the very simple model used by Ballentine, the development of realistic models capable of such a thorough analysis is a task for the future.[47]

---

[47] Asimakopulos and Burbidge analyze the short-run incidence of a profits tax in a model based on Kaleckian distribution theory instead of neoclassical theory on which the analyses discussed in the text are based. A. Asimakopulos and John B. Burbidge, "The Short-Period Incidence of Taxation," *The Economic Journal*, vol. 84 (June 1974), pp. 267-88. Since in Kaleckian's distribution theory there is no distinction between pure profits and normal profits, the analysis by Asimakopulos and Burbidge is thorough in the sense referred to in the text. They conclude that it is quite possible for 100 percent of the tax to be shifted. These conclusions stem from two very rigid assumptions, however: investment is fixed in the short run, and all savings come from profits. Since savings must be equal to investment, if the share of profits saved is constant, then after-tax profits must be constant, which implies that a tax increase must be completely shifted. While the analysis by Asimakopulos and Burbidge is a bit more detailed and complex than the summary just given, nonetheless the essential natures of their model and their results are as just stated. Their acceptance of the somewhat rigid and highly controversial Kaleckian theory of the distribution of income is critical to their results. In particular, that theory implies that an increase in investment *plans* for a given year must raise profits in the same year to generate extra savings, even though the planned investments do not increase output until later years.

3

The Incidence of the Corporation Income Tax in the Long Run

Even if the burden of the corporate income tax falls on stockholders in the short run, the long-run burden is likely to be spread to other agents in the economy. Such diffusion of the tax burden arises from a reduction in the capital stock in the corporate sector as well as a reduction in the economy's aggregate capital stock. The former reduction occurs as corporate investors choose to switch their investments to noncorporate ventures that are taxed at a relatively low rate, and the latter is the result of a reduction in total investment caused by a decline in the normal return to capital as well as a rise in the price of new investment goods.

Traditionally, a static model has been used for analysis of the effect of the reallocation of capital on the tax burden, while the effects of reduced investment have been examined by means of growth models. It is generally understood that a reallocation of capital between corporate and noncorporate ventures must actually take place in a growing economy; however, dealing with this process in a static model is a convenient expositional procedure. Accordingly, in the following section we examine the incidence of a corporation income tax in a static economy in which capital can easily be switched from employment in one sector to employment in another. In a later section we consider incidence in a growing economy.

Long-Run Incidence in a Static Economy

The seminal work on the incidence of the U.S. corporation income tax in a static economy is an article by Arnold Harberger published in 1962.[1] This article has attracted so much attention and been the basis

---

[1] Arnold C. Harberger, "The Incidence of the Corporation Income Tax," *Journal of Political Economy*, vol. 70 (June 1962), pp. 215-40.

for such a large amount of research that we will consider Harberger's analysis in some detail. In order to understand the rationale behind his approach, it is necessary to consider an earlier article by Harberger in which much of the empirical groundwork for the 1962 article was laid.[2] In the earlier work he showed that of the roughly $60 billion a year in returns to capital between 1953 and 1955, about $34 billion was corporate profits and $26 billion was other returns to capital. Approximately 80 percent of that $26 billion accrued to capital employed in agriculture and real estate. Further, for practical purposes all industries other than real estate, agriculture, and miscellaneous repair services paid more than 20 percent of their return to capital in corporation taxes, while those three industries paid less than 4 percent of their capital income in corporation income taxes.

Because of this apparently sharp division between industries that are dominated by corporations and industries dominated by firms that are not corporations, Harberger used a two-sector general equilibrium model in which one sector is made up of corporations producing a single product and the other sector is made up of noncorporate firms producing another product. Precisely why all firms producing one product should choose to incorporate while those producing another product should choose not to do so was not discussed by Harberger; the data suggesting that this is the case were taken as sufficient to justify his use of a two-sector model. As discussed in the next chapter, the decision whether or not to incorporate a firm is part of the broader question of a firm's optimal financial policy. For much of the remainder of this chapter we follow Harberger and take the corporate/noncorporate division of the economy as given. As before, we assume that firms do not adjust their financial policies when the corporate tax is imposed or altered.

Accepting, then, the simple division of the economy into two sectors, we can turn to the more particular assumptions of the Harberger model and the results that it suggests.[3] There have been a

---

[2] Arnold C. Harberger, "The Corporation Income Tax: An Empirical Appraisal," in U.S. House of Representatives, Ways and Means Committee, *Tax Revision Compendium* (Washington, D.C.: Government Printing Office, 1959), vol. 1, pp. 231-50. See also Leonard G. Rosenberg, "Taxation of Income from Capital, by Industry Group," in *The Taxation of Income from Capital*, ed. Arnold Harberger and Martin Bailey (Washington, D.C.: The Brookings Institution, 1969), pp. 123-84. The data discussed in these two articles cover the years 1953-1959.

[3] Harberger noted that the model which he used had been used for some time in the literature on international trade before he adopted it for tax analysis. Harberger, "Incidence of the Corporation Income Tax," p. 215. However, his was the first application of that model to tax analysis, and, as a result, in the public finance literature the model has come to be known as the Harberger model.

number of studies in which the nature of the Harberger model has been explained in considerable depth; a fairly simple summary of the model should therefore be sufficient here.[4] In the production side of the model it is assumed that all firms in the two sectors are perfect competitors and that their production functions have constant returns to scale. Further, firms obtain their capital and labor in competitive markets, and those factors of production can move freely from one sector to another. (It is this assumption of the mobility of capital that indicates the long-run nature of the model.)

On the demand side of the model it is assumed that the government and the private sector divide their expenditures between the two goods in exactly the same way. If government spending differs from that of the private sector, then a rise in tax revenues, no matter what particular tax is used, will cause an increase in the output of the good on which the government spends more than does the private sector and a decline in the output of the other good. In general, such a change in output will alter the wage rate, the rate of return to capital, and output prices. As mentioned, such effects arise no matter what particular tax is used, and, consequently, they are not really a part of the incidence of the tax in question. The assumption that the government and the private sector spend identically rules out any effects from differences in expenditure, so the remaining changes in prices and rates of return caused by a tax increase are the result of the particular tax used and are indicators of its incidence.[5]

---

[4] In his general survey of the literature on tax incidence, Mieszkowski discusses Harberger's model in some depth, as does Break; see Peter M. Mieszkowski, "Tax Incidence Theory: The Effects of Taxes on the Distribution of Income," *Journal of Economic Literature*, vol. 7 (December 1969), pp. 1103-24; and Break, "Incidence and Economic Effects of Taxation," pp. 129-34. McLure specifically reviews the literature in which Harberger's model is used; see Charles E. McLure, Jr., "General Equilibrium Incidence Analysis: The Harberger Model after Ten Years," *Journal of Public Economics*, vol. 4 (1975), pp. 125-61. Less technical discussions of the model can be found in Arnold C. Harberger, "Taxation: Corporation Income Taxes," in *International Encyclopedia of the Social Sciences*, ed. D. L. Sills (New York: Macmillan and Free Press, 1968), pp. 538-45, and Charles E. McLure, Jr. and Wayne R. Thirsk, "A Simplified Exposition of the Harberger Model; Part 1: Tax Incidence," *National Tax Journal*, vol. 28 (March 1975), pp. 1-27. Finally, McLure presents a graphical analysis based on Harberger's model under the assumption that labor is immobile, while Krauss and Johnson present a slightly different graphical analysis of a general form of the two-sector model; see Charles E. McLure, Jr., "A Diagrammatic Exposition of the Harberger Model," *Journal of Political Economy*, vol. 82 (1974), pp. 56-82, and Melvyn B. Krauss and Harry G. Johnson, "The Theory of Tax Incidence: A Diagrammatic Analysis," *Economica*, vol. 39 (November 1972), pp. 357-82.

[5] An alternative procedure, which Harberger did not follow, is to analyze the substitution of one tax for another while government expenditures are held

The model is static in the sense that the total supplies of capital and labor are taken to be fixed.[6] Further, wages and prices are sufficiently flexible that both factors of production are fully employed. Thus it is the allocation of resources rather than the overall level of resources utilization which is determined in the model. At first glance it may seem restrictive to ignore unemployment. However, the point of the analysis based on Harberger's model is to isolate the effect of one particular form of government finance, the corporation income tax, rather than to examine the effects of macroeconomic policies, such as changes in the total budget of the government or changes in the means of financing any government deficit. For the same reason, the model is designed to determine only *relative* prices. The absolute price level, and thus the rate of inflation, if any, is not given by the model.

Having briefly outlined the nature of Harberger's model, we can turn to the incidence results that it implies. The general issue here is whether or not the actual burden of the corporation income tax is the same as the statutory burden—that is, Is the tax paid by stockholders? It is convenient to divide this issue into two parts. First, is the tax borne only by capitalists who own corporate stock or do other capitalists bear a burden? Second, does any of the burden spread to consumers or to labor? The first of these questions can be answered rather quickly; indeed, the answer comes so quickly that its importance is easily underestimated. Since investors can move their capital freely between the corporate sector and the noncorporate sector, they will never accept a lower rate of return in one sector than is available in the other. As a consequence, it is impossible for the tax to reduce the net return paid to corporate investors below that paid to noncorporate investors. Though the tax legally falls on corporate profits, its burden at least spreads to noncorporate investors. The implication of this for the progressivity of the tax is quite important. If the burden is borne by all capitalists, then anyone who owns a home, a savings account, government bonds, or other noncorporate assets bears part of the burden of the corporation income tax. Clearly the resulting distribution of the burden will be much less progressive than it would be if the tax were borne only by stockholders.

---

constant. Clearly this avoids "contaminating" the results with the effect of a change in government expenditures, but it does necessitate dealing with the effect of the particular tax that is substituted for the corporation income tax.

[6] There is a further sense in which the model is static. The model can only be used to solve for the equilibrium prices and output levels which result from different tax policies. The movement of the economy from one equilibrium to another in the course of time is ignored.

There are two qualifications to this conclusion. One has to do with optimal corporate financial policy and will be taken up in Chapter 4. The other has to do with the realism of the assumed free mobility of physical capital. Obviously investors cannot repossess their share of a corporation's physical capital, change that capital into, say, a tractor, and then invest it in an unincorporated farm. But the mobility assumption should not be taken so literally. The real-world equivalent of the reallocation of capital is a diversion of *new* investment into noncorporate ventures instead of corporate stock. In that context it does not seem unrealistic to believe that ultimately rates of return after tax will be roughly equalized throughout the economy.

The answer to the second incidence question, Does any of the burden spread to labor or consumers? is more complex than the answer to the first. Indeed there is no general answer; the possibility and extent of such further diffusion of the burden depends on such matters as the capital intensities of the two sectors, elasticities of factor substitution in the two sectors, and price and income elasticities of demand. We first sketch the mechanism by which the burden may spread to labor and consumers, then review the numerical estimates of incidence that are based on realistic values for parameters such as those mentioned above.

In the short run, when capital is immobile, the corporation income tax will reduce the net return paid to corporate capitalists by the amount of the tax, leaving the corporate cost of capital and all other variables in the economy unchanged. It is this decline in the corporate net return that induces the long-run movement of capital into the noncorporate sector. The flow of capital into the noncorporate sector tends to reduce the marginal productivity of capital there, thus causing the return paid to noncorporate capitalists to decline. This process by itself tends to impose the burden of the tax only on capitalists; however, it leads to other adjustments that impose some burden on consumers and, perhaps, on workers as well.

In order to keep from losing all its capital, the corporate sector must increase the net return paid to capitalists to the level of that paid in the noncorporate sector. Corporations are able to do so because the outflow of capital increases the marginal product of that capital which remains in the corporate sector, thus raising the before-tax return that can be paid to capital there. Because of that rise in the corporate net return above the level to which it fell in the short run, however, the total cost of capital in the corporate sector must rise. Since corporations use marginal cost pricing this means that the price of corporate output rises. The tax-induced rise in the price of corporate output imposes a burden on all consumers. The decline in the net return paid to capitalists, however, reduces the noncorporate cost of capital and thus reduces the price of noncorporate goods, which in turn benefits consumers. Even given the benefit to consumers from the decline in the price of noncorporate output, the total effect of the change in the relative prices of products imposes a burden on consumers. This is because the rise in the price of corporate output in relation to the price of noncorporate output is solely due to the tax and does not reflect a true change in the cost to society of producing those two products. Stated more generally, the corporation income tax *artificially* increases the cost of capital to corporations. That cost increase manifests itself, at least partially, in a tax-induced rise in the price of corporate output relative to the price of noncorporate output. This distortion of relative product prices by the tax imposes a burden upon all consumers.

Thus far we have seen that the tax burden will be borne, not only by all capitalists, but also by all persons in their roles as consumers. However, part of the adjustment process remains to be discussed, and this part may impose a burden specifically on laborers. The increase in the price of corporate output will cause consumers to purchase more of the noncorporate product, which means an increase in noncorporate output and a consequent decrease in corporate output. Suppose that the corporate sector is more labor-intensive than the noncorporate sector—that is, that it has a lower capital–labor ratio. Then the flow of capital *and* labor from the corporate sector to the noncorporate sector induced by the changes in output will reduce the ratio of capital to labor in both sectors.[7] Since the capital–labor ratio decreases in both sectors, the marginal productivity of labor declines and, consequently, the wage rate declines in relation to the return paid to capital. In this case, then, there is a tendency for some of the burden to be spread to labor. If the corporate sector is capital-intensive, there is no tendency for labor to bear a burden—except, of course, that workers, like capitalists, bear some burden as consumers of corporate output.

Just what the ultimate incidence of the tax will be depends upon many particular factors in the economy such as: the price elasticity of demand for corporate output, which determines how large a shift in

---

[7] Proof of this statement is fairly technical, and a numerical example will be sufficient here. Suppose that in the corporate sector there are ten units of capital and a hundred of labor, while in the noncorporate sector there are fifty of each. The capital intensity of the flow of capital and labor will be between that of the two sectors. Specifically, suppose that one unit of capital and five units of labor flow out of the corporate sector into the noncorporate sector. This reduces the corporate capital–labor ratio from 1/10 to 9/95 and the noncorporate ratio from 1/1 to 51/55.

outputs is caused by the rise in the corporate price; the elasticities of factor substitution in the two sectors, which determine how sensitive relative factor rewards are to changes in capital–labor ratios; and the capital intensities of the two sectors, the importance of which has just been discussed. Using his model and data on the U.S. economy for 1953–1955, as well as a range of reasonable values for the various elasticities, Harberger calculated the approximate incidence of the U.S. corporation income tax. His calculations show consistently that capitalists bear approximately 100 percent of the direct burden of the tax.[8]

These numerical results are best interpreted in the light of a theorem proved by Harberger. He showed that if both production functions are Cobb-Douglas functions and if a constant fraction of income is spent on each good, then, no matter which sector is capital-intensive, capitalists bear *exactly* 100 percent of the direct tax burden. Harberger's numerical calculations show that even if the production functions are not quite Cobb-Douglas—specifically, that if the elasticities of factor substitution range between -0.5 and -1.2—and the price elasticity of demand for the corporate good is not precisely equal to -1, which it is if a constant share of income is spent on each good, then stockholders and noncorporate capitalists still bear virtually the full burden of the tax.

As might be expected, the derivation of such a strong conclusion from what is ultimately a very simple model of a complex economy stimulated a large amount of work in which the attempt has been made to make the model more "realistic" and to determine the sensitivity of the results to plausible changes in the basic assumptions. One of the most important and restrictive of Harberger's assumptions is the statement that the economy does not grow. We defer discussion of corporate tax incidence in growing economies until the next section, however, and now consider instead modifications of Harberger's work in which the assumption of a static economy has been retained. Within that context it appears that Harberger's results are quite robust.

There are three salient features of Harberger's analysis that have attracted considerable interest, either because of their restrictive nature or because they seem quite unrealistic. First, since the corporate sector includes many very large firms that have significant shares of their product markets, Harberger's assumption that firms in that sector

---

[8] As will be discussed in Chapter 5, the tax imposes an excess burden that is borne throughout the economy. Because of the excess burden, and because of the possibility that the tax actually makes laborers better off, capitalists can suffer a loss of income that is greater than the gain in revenue by the government. In such an instance, capitalists are said to bear more than 100 percent of the tax burden.

behave as perfect competitors is implausible. In the appendix to his 1962 article, Harberger himself modifies his model to take into account monopoly elements in the corporate sector.[9] He adopts a rather simple rule of behavior for corporations; they are assumed to charge a price that is a fixed markup over average costs, which include the normal return to capital and the tax on that return. In spite of this change in the model, he still finds that a tax on the normal rate of return to capital is borne entirely by capitalists. Anderson and Ballentine extend Harberger's analysis of this case by generalizing the fixed markup pricing behavioral rule.[10] They assume that firms in the corporate sector face downward-sloping demand curves and maximize their pure profits subject to those demand curves. In their analysis, the corporation income tax is assessed against the firm's pure profits and the normal rate of return paid to capitalists. The incidence results in this model, in which imperfect competition is assumed, are almost identical to those obtained under the assumption of perfect competition. To see why this is so, it is useful to treat the corporation income tax as two taxes, one that is a tax only on pure profits and one that is a tax on the normal return to capital. Since corporations are assumed to maximize pure profits, the tax on pure profits is borne entirely by the recipients of those profits. This part of the tax burden is not spread to all capitalists.

In the long run, capital is perfectly mobile; thus the tax on normal profits is simply a tax on part of the variable costs of a firm. Its effect is essentially the same whether or not firms have monopoly power. In particular, the tax causes an outflow of capital from the corporate sector in order to equate the *normal* returns to capital after tax.[11] This outflow causes the rate of return to capital to decline. Further, the marginal cost curves of corporations shift upward, their output declines, and the resulting outflow of capital and labor increases or decreases the capital–labor ratio in each sector depending, as before, upon the relative capital intensity of the two sectors. The extent to which these two adjustments occur is affected somewhat by the fact that in the model in which imperfect competition is assumed,

---

[9] Harberger, "Incidence of the Corporation Income Tax," pp. 238-40.

[10] Robert Anderson and J. Gregory Ballentine, "The Incidence and Excess Burden of a Profits Tax under Imperfect Competition," *Public Finance*, vol. 31, no. 2 (1976), pp. 159-76.

[11] In maximizing pure profits, monopolies pay only the normal return to capital at the margin. The pure profits are an inframarginal rent. Consequently, the short-run decline in the normal return to capital after the tax is imposed still acts as an impetus for marginal capitalists to shift their capital to the noncorporate sector.

corporate firms are equating marginal cost and marginal revenue, while in the original Harberger model they equate marginal cost and price; however, the results are not greatly affected by this difference. Over all, even if corporations possess monopoly power, the decline in total corporate and noncorporate profits in the long run is roughly equal to 100 percent of tax revenues.

The second feature of Harberger's analysis that has attracted a great deal of attention is a rather technical one. Mathematically, Harberger's procedure was to specify the equations describing his model, differentiate those equations, then solve the model for the formula for the derivative of the rate of return to capital with respect to the tax rate. Among the parameters of the formula are factor shares, elasticities of factor substitution, and elasticities of demand. Using data on corporate and noncorporate factor shares and a range of values for the various elasticities, Harberger calculated values for that derivative and used those values to provide a linear approximation of the effect of a finite tax change on the rate of return to capital.[12] Such linear approximations can be expected to be accurate for small tax changes, but whether they are accurate for predicting the effect of such a large change as abolition of the entire U.S. corporation income tax is a serious issue.

Using Scarf's algorithm for the calculation of economic equilibria, John Shoven and John Whalley have virtually resolved this issue, and their resolution has shown that Harberger's incidence calculations are quite accurate.[13] Scarf's algorithm allows calculation of the exact equilibrium values of all prices, outputs, and rates of return in an economy on the basis of knowledge of production functions, demand functions, factor endowments, and tax rates. Shoven and Whalley

---

[12] The issue surrounding the use of linear approximations should not be confused with the zero tax restrictions of Harberger's original model. Because Harberger omits income effects from the demand equation, his solution of the model gives the formula for the derivative of the rate of return with respect to the tax when the tax rate is zero. If the tax rate is not zero, the formula is incomplete. This matter is discussed in J. Gregory Ballentine and Ibrahim Eris, "On the General Equilibrium Analysis of Tax Incidence," *Journal of Political Economy*, vol. 83 (June 1975), pp. 633-44. They derive the general formula for that derivative which is valid for all corporate tax rates. While that general formula can be used to derive *qualitative* theorems of the incidence of finite taxes, the numerical estimates based on it are linear approximations and, accordingly, are subject to the type of error mentioned in the text.

[13] See John Shoven and John Whalley, "A General Equilibrium Calculation of the Effect of Differential Taxation of Income from Capital in the U.S.," *Journal of Public Economics*, vol. 1 (November 1972), pp. 281-321; and John Shoven, "The Incidence and Efficiency Effects of Taxes on Income from Capital," *Journal of Political Economy*, vol. 84 (December 1976), pp. 1261-83.

used that algorithm to compute the rate of return that would have prevailed in the Harberger model if the corporation income tax had been abolished. As a result, they avoided the use of linear approximations and calculated the exact incidence of the tax in that model. For calculations based on the same elasticity parameters, the linear approximations are very close to the exact calculation.[14] The use of more sophisticated, accurate techniques thus does not alter the fundamental conclusion: in the Harberger model capitalists bear virtually 100 percent of the tax.

Finally, it is obviously important to determine whether or not the level of aggregation affects the results significantly. If many more than two sectors are considered, analytical solutions such as that obtained by Harberger become extremely complex. Using the Scarf algorithm, however, it is comparatively easy to disaggregate the model. Shoven has done so with the use of twelve sectors, three of which are noncorporate, or low-tax, sectors and nine of which are corporate, or high-tax, sectors.[15] His results show clearly that for similar elasticity values the twelve-sector incidence results are quite close to the two-sector results. Indeed, Shoven's preferred estimate indicates that capitalists bear 103 percent of the tax burden.[16]

In an ambitious project that is still in progress, Fullerton, Shoven, and Whalley are constructing a general equilibrium model with nineteen sectors, twelve income classes, intermediate products, and a wealth of detail on various aspects of the U.S. economy, including a careful modeling of the U.S. tax system.[17] Their primary concern has been the excess burden of taxation; however, their results are con-

[14] For example, if the elasticity of substitution in demand is −0.5 and both elasticities of factor substitution are −1, then the linear approximation result is that profits fall by an amount equal to 111 percent of the tax revenues; the exact calculations show profits falling by an amount equal to about 118 percent of the tax revenues. If the elasticities of demand and of factor substitution in the corporate sector are both −1 and the elasticity of factor substitution in the noncorporate sector is −0.5, then both procedures show profits falling by an amount equal to about 117 percent of tax revenues. These linear approximation values are slight corrections of Harberger's calculations and are presented in Ballentine and Eris, "On the General Equilibrium Analysis," p. 641. The exact calculations are from Shoven, "The Incidence and Efficiency Effects," pp. 1276-77.

[15] Shoven, "The Incidence and Efficiency Effects," pp. 1279-81.

[16] Ibid., pp. 1280-81.

[17] See Don Fullerton, John Shoven, and John Whalley, "General Equilibrium Analysis of U.S. Taxation Policy," in U.S. Department of the Treasury, 1978 Compendium of Tax Research (Washington, D.C., 1978), pp. 23-58; and Don Fullerton, John Shoven, and John Whalley, "General Equilibrium Impacts of Replacing the U.S. Income Tax with a Progressive Consumption Tax," paper presented at the North American Meetings of the Econometric Society, Chicago, August 31, 1978.

sistent with the conclusion of the two-sector model that the burden of the extra tax on corporate profits falls primarily on all capitalists. One of the particular advantages of the work of Fullerton, Shoven, and Whalley is their explicit inclusion of twelve different income groups. They are able to show how the diffusion of the tax burden distributes that burden among all income classes.

While some alternative assumptions can certainly be devised which when applied to Harberger's model can alter the essential results, it does appear that those results are applicable to a wide range of plausible conditions.[18] One potentially significant modification of the assumptions of the model that has not been extensively explored is allowance for variability in the total supply of capital through international mobility of capital. If a tax increase causes an initial decline in the rate of return paid to capital of, say, 10 percent, and if that decline causes a flow of capital out of the United States into other countries, then the ratio of capital to labor in the United States will decline, the marginal productivity of capital will rise, and the net return paid to capital will also rise. Thus, after the flow of capital has been completed, the tax actually causes the net return to fall less than 10 percent.[19] A useful and realistic modeling of international flows of physical capital is quite difficult because of the complex tax treatment of the income of foreign capital in the United States and other countries. Apart from this qualification concerning the potential importance of international capital mobility, the work generalizing Harberger's model seems to indicate that if the economy is a static one in which some industries may be imperfectly competitive, firms maximize profits, capital is mobile between sectors, and the distribution of income is determined in accord with standard neoclassical economic theory, then a tax on the profits earned in certain industries will be borne largely by those who earn profits in all sectors of the

[18] Batra has shown that some of the analytical properties of the Harberger model change if there is uncertainty over prices or outputs. Unfortunately, it is not clear from his work whether these differences are significant. See R. W. Batra, "A General Equilibrium Model of the Incidence of the Corporation Income Tax under Uncertainty," *Journal of Public Economics*, vol. 4 (November 1975), pp. 343-60. In addition, Ratti and Shome have modified the Harberger model so as to include a third factor of production, land. When they evaluate their solution numerically, using very high elasticity of substitution parameters for land, they find that capitalists escape much of the burden and that it is borne instead by landowners. See Suresh P. Ratti and Parthasarathi Shome, "The Incidence of the Corporation Income Tax: A Long Run, Specific Factor Model," *Southern Economic Journal*, vol. 44 (July 1977), pp. 85-98.

[19] If capital is perfectly mobile internationally, then the flow of capital will prevent the net return from falling at all, and capitalists will not bear any of the tax burden. Instead, the burden will be shared by labor and consumers.

economy. It is generally acknowledged, however, that the movement of capital between sectors must actually take place in a growing economy. Accordingly, conclusions as to the long-run incidence of a tax on profits must be based on models of growing economies.

The Incidence of the Corporate Tax in Growing Economies

The essential difference between tax incidence in static economies and tax incidence in growing economies is the effect of the tax on investment and the aggregate ratio of capital to labor. In a closed, static economy, the aggregate capital stock is exogenously given, and the supply of labor is either dependent on a choice between labor and leisure or is also exogenously given. In models of growing economies, labor is usually taken to grow at a fixed rate while the stock of capital is determined by investment decisions made in the past. In such an economy a tax change can influence investment, and, consequently, a tax change can alter the equilibrium capital–labor ratio in the economy.

In order to understand the possible effect of a tax-induced change in the aggregate capital–labor ratio on tax incidence, it will be useful first to review briefly what is meant by an equilibrium growth path and how the economy moves toward such a growth path in a simple, taxless world. Suppose that there is a single output, Q, which can be used either for consumption or for investment. Let s denote the proportion of Q that is saved and let I denote investment. Then,

$$sQ = I.$$

If the production function for Q exhibits constant returns to scale, that production function can then be written in intensity form as

$$Q/K = f(L/K) \qquad\qquad f' > 0$$

where K is capital and L is labor. If labor grows at a constant rate, n, then long-run growth equilibrium requires that the *rate* of growth of capital be equal to n;[20] that is,

$$I/K = n.$$

If this condition is satisfied, then labor and capital grow at the same rate, so the aggregate capital–labor ratio is constant, the capital–output ratio is constant, and the wage rate in relation to the rate of return

---

[20] For expositional convenience, we are assuming that there is no depreciation. The general topic of the tax treatment of depreciation will be taken up in Chapter 4.

to capital is constant.[21] We have implicitly chosen Q to be the numeraire good, so the price of Q is always constant.

It is the method by which the economy adjusts to attain the equilibrium growth path and the consequences of that adjustment which are particularly important for analysis of tax incidence. Suppose that the rate of saving, s, is constant and that initially the ratio of output to capital, Q/K, is such that

$$sQ/K = I/K < n.$$

If this is the case, labor grows faster than capital does; thus the capital–labor ratio declines and the output–capital ratio rises, moving the economy toward equilibrium. As the capital–labor ratio declines during the movement toward equilibrium, the marginal product of capital relative to the marginal product of labor rises, and, therefore, the rate of return to capital rises relative to the wage rate. As will be seen, this adjustment in relative returns is a crucial aspect of long-run incidence.

We can now turn to an explicit analysis of the incidence of a tax on profits in a growing economy. For the moment we will continue to assume that only a single good, Q, is produced.[22] Firms producing Q are all corporations and are perfect competitors. The aggregate savings rate is the weighted average of the savings rates of labor, capitalists, and the government—that is,

$$s = s_w(wL/Q) + s_\pi(rK/Q) + S_R(rtK/Q)$$

where s_w is labor's savings rate, s_π is capitalists' savings rate, S_R is the government savings rate, w is the wage rate, r is the after-tax rate of return to capital, and t is the tax rate.[23]

---

[21] The latter condition arises from the fact that, with a production function in which the return to scale is constant, the wage rate in relation to the rate of return to capital is a function of the capital–labor ratio alone.

[22] The bulk of the studies of the incidence of taxes on profits in a growing economy use one-sector models. See, for example, Marian Krzyzaniak, "The Long-Run Burden of a General Tax on Profits in a Neo-classical World," *Public Finance*, vol. 22 (1967), pp. 472-91; Marian Krzyzaniak, "Factor Substitution and the General Tax on Profits," *Public Finance*, vol. 25 (1970), pp. 489-514; Martin Feldstein, "Tax Incidence in a Growing Economy with Variable Factor Supply," *Quarterly Journal of Economics*, vol. 88 (November 1974), pp. 551-73; and Martin Feldstein, "The Incidence of a Capital Income Tax in a Growing Economy with Variable Savings Rates," *Review of Economic Studies*, vol. 41 (October 1974), pp. 505-13. Krzyzaniak also discusses tax incidence in a two-sector economy; for his actual calculations, however, he aggregates the economy to a one-sector model. Marian Krzyzaniak, "The Burden of a Differential Tax on Profits in a Neo-classical World," *Public Finance*, vol. 23 (1968), pp. 447-73.

[23] For convenience, the tax rate is expressed as a fraction of net of tax returns. What is normally referred to as a 50 percent tax on profits would imply $t = 1$ in the above formulation.

If it is assumed initially that the rate of savings by each group is constant, then the long-run incidence of the tax depends on whether or not those savings rates are the same for labor, capitalists, and the government. In the period when the tax is imposed, capital is in fixed supply; thus its return is a quasi-rent and capitalists initially bear the full burden of the tax—that is, rK falls by the same amount that rtK, government revenues, rises. If capitalists and the government save at the same rate, then this redistribution of income will have no effect on the aggregate savings rate, the economy will not be jarred out of long-run equilibrium, and capitalists must bear the full burden of the tax in the long run as well as in the short run. Note that with savings rates constant and $s_\pi = S_R$, the value of the rate of saving by labor is irrelevant to the above analysis.

Consider, however, an alternative situation that is commonly assumed in the literature, one in which laborers and capitalists save, but the government does not—that is, s_w and s_π are positive, but $S_R = 0$.[24] In this case, the transfer of income to the government lowers the aggregate savings rate so that $s(Q/K) < n$ and the economy is out of long-run equilibrium. Equilibrium is restored by the process discussed above: the capital–labor ratio declines and the rate of return to capital before tax rises relative to the wage rate. The rise in the before-tax return to capital implies that the net return rises above the level to which it fell in the short run. In other words, through this process capitalists avoid the full burden of the tax in the long run, and some of it is borne by labor.[25] How much of the tax burden is

---

[24] See, for example, Feldstein, "The Incidence of a Capital Income Tax in a Growing Economy," p. 506; and Krzyzaniak, "The Long-Run Burden of a General Tax on Profits," p. 48.

[25] A way of measuring tax burdens in a growing economy must be chosen with care. For example, consider two economies which are identical except that in one of them a tax on profits was imposed fifty years ago while the other economy is taxless. Profits in the economy with a tax will be less than those in the other economy for two reasons: the net rate of return is lower, and the capital stock is lower. A simple calculation of the difference in total profits between the two economies is a misleading indicator of the burden laid upon capitalists. While the lower rate of return in the taxed economy is a true burden on capitalists, the smaller stock of capital is not. The fact that the capital stock in the taxed economy is smaller than that in the untaxed economy fifty years after the imposition of a tax implies that in previous years consumption in the taxed economy was greater. Consequently, the smaller stock of capital is not a true burden. On this point, see Martin Feldstein, "Tax Incidence in a Growing Economy with Variable Factor Supply," p. 565. Krzyzaniak prefers to include changes in the stock of capital in his calculations of tax burden; his rationale is discussed in "The Long-Run Burden of a General Tax on Profits," pp. 472-77. As will be discussed in Chapter 5, the reduction in the stock of capital does impose an *excess burden* borne by the economy as a whole.

spread to labor depends upon the relative sizes of s_w and s_π, the elasticity of factor substitution, and the share of labor in national income. Calculations by Feldstein for using plausible values of these parameters indicate that considerable shifting in the long run is likely.[26]

The basic impetus to long-run shifting in the case just described comes from the transfer of income away from the private sector, where some income is saved, to the government sector, where there is no saving. Much the same process would occur if government revenues increased by means of a payroll tax, a consumption tax, or any other tax. In order to isolate the effect of the tax in question, it is preferable to assume that the rate of saving by the government is the same as that in the private sector.[27] This is in essence similar to Harberger's assumption in his static model that consumption by the government is the same as that by the private sector.

As discussed above, if the rate of saving by the government is taken to be the same as that by capitalists, and if that rate is constant, then from the one-sector model it can be seen that capitalists bear the full burden of the tax in the long run. If rates of saving decline when the interest rate declines, however, and there is evidence that such is the case, once again a considerable share of the burden of a tax on profits will be borne by workers.[28] This happens because, when there

[26] Feldstein, "The Incidence of a Capital Income Tax in a Growing Economy," p. 507. Krzyzaniak, in "The Long-Run Burden of a General Tax on Profits," also finds that labor bears a significant burden in the long run.

[27] Alternatively, what is called a differential incidence approach can be followed—that is, the substitution of one tax for another, leaving government revenues unchanged, can be examined. While this requires dealing with the effects of two taxes simultaneously, it does permit avoidance of the effect of differences between patterns of spending and saving by the government and those of the private sector. Feldstein followed a differential incidence approach in the latter half of his article, "The Incidence of a Capital Income Tax in a Growing Economy," pp. 508-10.

[28] There are a fair number of studies of the effect of interest rates on savings. These studies give conflicting results, however. For a brief critical review of recent studies, see George M. von Furstenberg and Burton G. Malkiel, "The Government and Capital Formation: A Study of Recent Issues," Journal of Economic Literature, vol. 15 (September 1977), pp. 840-42. A recent careful study that has attracted considerable interest is Michael J. Boskin, "Taxation, Saving, and the Rate of Interest," Journal of Political Economy, vol. 86 Supplement (April 1978), pp. S3-S27. Boskin finds that the interest elasticity of savings is 0.4. This general result is supported in Michael J. Boskin and Lawrence J. Lau, "Taxation and Aggregate Factor Supply: Preliminary Estimates," in U.S. Department of the Treasury, 1978 Compendium of Tax Research. However, Boskin's results have been severely criticized on the ground that they are quite sensitive to the interest rate series used in the analysis. For a discussion of this criticism and a defense of Boskin's results, see E. Philip Howrey and Saul H. Hymans, "The Measurement and Determination of Loanable Funds Savings," and the subsequent discussion in Brookings Papers on Economic Activity 3:1978, pp. 655-705.

is a positive relationship between savings and the return on savings, and the tax reduces that return, savings decline. As before, the decline in total savings jars the economy out of long-run equilibrium, and equilibrium is restored only when the capital–labor ratio and the wage rate decline. Feldstein's analysis of the substitution of a tax on profits for a payroll tax indicates that if the savings rate of all agents in the economy is the same, the production function is a Cobb-Douglas function, and the elasticity of savings with respect to the interest rate is around 0.3 or 0.4, then 25 to 29 percent of the long-run burden of a tax on profits may be shifted to labor.[29] If the rate of saving by capitalists is greater than that of labor, even more shifting is indicated.

The analysis has so far been concerned primarily with the effect on savings of the imposition of the tax. If the tax reduces savings, either through a transfer of income from those who save more to those who save less or through a reduction in all savings rates because of the tax-induced decline in the rate of return to capital, then at least part of the tax burden will be shifted. In the simple one-sector model which we have used—and that has been used in the bulk of the literature on incidence in growing economies—the only long-run adjustment to the tax comes through changes in aggregate savings. However, another way in which the tax can lead to adjustments in the growth of the economy, and some shifting of the tax in the long run, is through an increase in the price of new investment goods. In order to examine such a possibility, it is necessary to use at least a two-sector growth model.

In what is a fairly natural generalization of Harberger's static analysis, Ballentine used a two-sector growth model to examine the incidence of a corporation income tax.[30] Since Harberger's empirical

---

[29] Feldstein, "The Incidence of a Capital Income Tax in a Growing Economy," p. 509. Diamond analyzes tax incidence in a two-generation growth model. Since savings behavior is endogenous in that model, it is difficult to impose specific elasticities of savings on it in order to obtain estimates of incidence. His results do indicate a reduction in saving, however, and a consequent shifting of the tax burden onto labor. Peter Diamond, "Incidence of an Interest Income Tax," Journal of Economic Theory, vol. 2 (September 1972), pp. 211-29.

[30] J. Gregory Ballentine, "The Incidence of a Corporation Income Tax in a Growing Economy," Journal of Political Economy, vol. 86 (October 1978), pp. 863-76. Friedlaender and Vandendorpe have also used a two-sector growth model to examine the incidence of a capital income tax in one sector. Ann F. Friedlaender and Adolf L. Vandendorpe, "Capital Taxation in a Dynamic General Equilibrium Setting," Journal of Public Economics, vol. 10 (August 1978), pp. 1-24. In the interests of achieving greater realism, Friedlaender and Vandendorpe introduced a number of complicating features into their model, such as a supply of money and the potential for financing by means of government bonds. These realistic attributes of their model make the generality of their results difficult to

results indicate that the manufacturing sector is included in the corporate sector, Ballentine assumed that output of the corporate sector can be used either for consumption or for new capital goods, while output of the noncorporate sector—largely agriculture, real estate, and some services—can be used only for consumption. This means that the nature of the output of the corporate sector is essentially the same as the nature of the output of the single sector in one-sector growth models such as those discussed above.

To see what additional information is gained from the two-sector growth model, write the part of the output of the corporate sector that is used for new capital goods as X^I and the price of all corporate output as P_x. Total savings, S, are equal to total *expenditures* on new capital goods; thus:

$$S = P_x X^I.$$

As before, long-run equilibrium requires that capital and labor grow at the same rate; that is, the long-run equilibrium condition is

$$X^I/K = n,$$

where K and n are as defined above.

In this model, the initial effect of imposing a corporation income tax is essentially the same as the effect of such a tax in Harberger's static model. Thus, it is known that initially the tax will reduce the net return to capital, increase the cost of capital to corporations, increase their marginal costs, and, therefore, cause their price, P_x, to rise.[31] Even if the rates of saving by the government and the private sector are identical and are unchanged by the decline in the rate of return to capital—that is, even if savings, S, do not decline when the tax is imposed—physical investment must decline. Because of the rise in the price of new capital goods, a constant level of savings purchases fewer capital goods.[32] Consequently, the rate of growth of capital (X^I/K) falls below that of labor. As happens when there is a decline in savings, equilibrium is restored through a decline in the capital to

---

understand, and specific results must rely upon numerical simulations. As Friedlaender and Vandendorpe stress, realistic simulations based on a model such as theirs are not possible now.

[31] This is because in the design of the growth model it was assumed that capital is completely mobile in each period. This is an unrealistic simplifying assumption; relaxing it, however, would probably not alter the basic results.

[32] Note that even if the entire corporation income tax is shifted forward in the short run so that the rate of return on savings does not decline and there is thus no reason to expect savings to decline, investment still declines. The forward shifting of the tax increases the price of capital goods and reduces the quantity of such goods that can be purchased out of a given level of savings.

labor ratio that increases the rate of return to capital relative to the wage rate, thus shifting some of the tax burden. Ballentine calculated that if savings are constant, some 15 to 30 percent of the burden of the tax may be shifted in the long run simply because of the increase in the cost of new capital goods.[33]

In general, the effect of the increase in the price of new investment goods reinforces the effect of a decline in savings caused by a decline in the return on savings—that is, physical investment declines, not only because a given level of savings purchases fewer new capital goods, but also because savings themselves decline. Using Boskin's estimate of the elasticity of savings with respect to the interest rate, Ballentine found that the total effect is such that 50 to 80 percent of the initial burden borne by capitalists is shifted to labor in the long run.[34] This suggests that the bulk of the tax on the income of stockholders may not be borne by stockholders, nor by capitalists in general, but by labor.

Summary

In analyses of long-run incidence, two adjustments have been pointed out by means of which part of the burden of the corporation income tax on stockholders can be shifted to other agents in the economy. The first is a reallocation of capital from the corporate sector to the noncorporate sector; the second is a reduction in the aggregate stock of capital. The intersectoral reallocation of capital spreads the burden to all capitalists, while the reduction in the stock of capital spreads the burden further to laborers. The fundamental conclusion to be drawn from studies of the long-run incidence of the corporation income tax is that even if firms do maximize their profits, the burden of the corporation income tax is not borne entirely by stockholders; instead, its burden is spread throughout the economy.

Consequently, these studies suggest that the corporation income tax is not a sharply progressive tax, as it would be if it were borne by stockholders alone. Instead, the burden of it is so diffused among stockholders, investors in noncorporate enterprises, consumers, and workers that it is difficult to predict any clear pattern of the incidence of the tax by income class. Before much confidence can be placed in such a conclusion, however, it is necessary to consider the results of

---

[33] Ballentine, "Incidence of a Corporation Income Tax in a Growing Economy," p. 872.
[34] Ibid.

some very recent literature in which the financial policies that firms can follow in order to avoid the corporation income tax are stressed. As will be seen in the next chapter, under some fairly stringent circumstances such policies can have the result that the tax is borne entirely by stockholders, even in the long run.

4

Corporate Financial Policy and Tax Incidence

The two preceding chapters dealt with a tax that is assessed against the total profits earned by a firm. The essential effect of such a tax, particularly its long-run effect, is derived from the fact that the tax increases the marginal cost of capital to corporations and decreases the after-tax return on new investment. The first of these induces both the flow of capital from the corporate sector to the noncorporate sector and the increase in the price of new capital goods. The second may cause investment to decline if rates of saving decline when the rate of return on investment declines. Recently there has been a considerable amount of analysis in which it is explicitly recognized that the tax falls only on equity profits net of depreciation and that interest payments are not included in the tax base. When this is taken into account, it is clear that the effect of the tax on the marginal cost of capital depends upon the way in which a firm finances its capital stock, and in particular it depends upon the extent to which new investments are financed by debt. Another way of putting this is that the effective tax rate on capital is an endogenous variable that can be reduced by the financial policies of firms. Indeed, it has been shown that under certain circumstances, firms will adjust their financial policies so radically that the effective tax on new capital becomes zero and the corporation income tax will thus not increase the marginal cost of capital to corporations. While the set of circumstances that will produce such an extreme result is unlikely to prevail in reality, in a more realistic setting the consequences of firms' adjusting their financial policies in response to tax changes is still important in the determination of tax incidence.

Taxation and Corporate Financial Policy

Initially, we will consider the choice by a firm of an optimal ratio of debt to equity in a taxless world. This will help to set the stage for the issue in which we are primarily interested: the interrelationship between the corporation income tax and the financial policy of a firm. Even in the absence of taxes, the determination of an optimal ratio of debt to equity is a complex issue. For some time the prevalent view was that in the absence of taxes an optimal financial policy exists. The argument justifying such a conclusion went something like the following: since interest payments are a virtually certain stream of income, while dividends and retentions are a residual paid out of uncertain total profits after interest payments have been made, it is reasonable to assume that equity investors would require a higher risk premium than bondholders. Suppose that equity holders require a 10 percent return and bondholders require only 7 percent. Consider a firm financed entirely by equity. That firm will choose to pursue all investment projects that have an expected return of 10 percent or more. However, the stockholders can increase their potential income if the firm uses debt to finance additional investment projects with expected returns of, say, 9 percent. The firm can use 7 of the 9 percent expected return to pay the interest on the debt and pay the remaining 2 percent to stockholders. Consequently, it is not in the best interest of the firm to use equity finance alone.

However, the argument continues, there is a limit to how much debt finance is desirable. As more debt finance is used, there is a larger fixed amount of interest that must be paid out of the uncertain stream of profits. As a result, equity income becomes riskier and the risk premium that must be paid on equity rises. The optimal ratio of debt to equity is one at which the advantages of the low rate of interest on debt are just offset by the effect of additional debt in increasing equity-risk premiums.

Modigliani and Miller pointed out that the above argument is misleading since it ignores the adjustments that the individual investor can make in his portfolio.[1] They argue that each investor can always adjust his own portfolio so that the financial policy of the corporation is irrelevant to its valuation by investors and that there is thus no optimal ratio of debt to equity. To see how this can come about, assume for the moment that bankruptcy is impossible and consider

---

[1] Franco Modigliani and Merton H. Miller, "The Cost of Capital, Corporation Finance, and the Theory of Investment," *American Economic Review*, vol. 48 (June 1958), pp. 261-97.

an investor who owns 10 percent of the total market value of a firm.[2] In particular, suppose that that firm has a fifty–fifty debt–equity ratio and that the investor owns exactly 10 percent of the debt and 10 percent of the equity of the firm. This investor will earn exactly 10 percent of the total profits of the firm. If profits are relatively low in a given year, most of those earnings will be in the form of interest payments, while if profits are high, most will be in the form of dividends or retentions. The risk position of this investor is exactly the same as that of an investor who holds 10 percent of the equity in an identical firm which is, however, financed entirely by equity.

To carry this example further, suppose that the firm with a fifty–fifty debt–equity ratio raises its debt–equity ratio to eighty–twenty. The investor who owns 10 percent of the firm can counteract this change in corporate financial policy simply by adjusting his own portfolio—that is, by increasing his holdings of the firm's bonds and reducing his equity holdings in such a way that he continues to own 10 percent of the firm's debt and 10 percent of its equity. As before, the investor will receive exactly 10 percent of the total earnings of the firm. Clearly, the change in the firm's debt–equity ratio has had no effect on the risk position of this investor; indeed, the firm's debt–equity ratio is irrelevant to his risk position. If the investor in question wished to have a riskier portfolio, he could hold 20 percent of the firm's equity and no debt or, if he wanted a more certain stream of income, he could hold 20 percent of the firm's debt and no equity. What the firm's debt–equity ratio is does not make any difference; the risk position of an individual investor is determined by his individual portfolio.

This is not the complete Modigliani-Miller theorem. Recall from the brief summary given above of work that preceded the analyses of Modigliani and Miller the argument that the firm will borrow at low interest rates to finance investments and return the excess of earnings over interest to its stockholders. It was the increase in risk premiums on equity as debt increased that limited this tendency. But if, as Modigliani and Miller argued, risk premiums do not respond to changes in the firm's debt–equity ratio, then why should the firm not borrow as much as possible? As before, it is important to take into account the behavior of the individual investor. If it is advantageous to stockholders for the firm to finance investments by borrowing, then as long as those stockholders borrow at the same rate of interest as firms do—an important assumption of the Modigliani-Miller

---

[2] Actually, it is only necessary to assume that there are no costs such as legal fees or transactions costs associated with bankruptcy.

theorem—then it is equally advantageous to the stockholders to borrow the money themselves and to purchase more stock to finance the investment. Individual borrowing is a perfect substitute for corporate borrowing. As a simplified example, consider an investor who owns 5 percent of the equity in a firm. Suppose that that firm intends to finance a new investment. If the firm borrows in order to finance the investment, then the investor in question will earn 5 percent of the excess of the return on the new investment above the interest rate. If, instead, the firm decides to issue new stock, then the investor can simply borrow enough to buy 5 percent of the new stock, and he will then earn 5 percent of the return on the new investment in excess of the interest rate that he pays. As long as the investor and the firm borrow at the same rate of interest, the method of financing the new investment is irrelevant. Note that personal income taxes and corporate income taxes are both ignored in this argument.

In summary then, as long as there are no taxes and there is no possibility of bankruptcy, the financial policy of the firm is irrelevant to its valuation—that is, no optimal financial policy exists. It is clear, however, that the assumption that there are no taxes is far too restrictive for an analysis of the financial policy of modern corporations. Modigliani and Miller realized this and showed how their conclusion would change if there was a corporation income tax.[3] The corporation income tax puts a penalty on equity financing that cannot be undone by the individual investor. Since, in the absence of taxes, firms are indifferent as to whether they finance by debt or by equity, even a very small tax that penalizes the firm for using one form of finance will cause the firm to use the other as much as possible. Modigliani and Miller concluded that in the presence of the corporation income tax, therefore, all firms would seek as high a ratio of debt to equity as possible. This conclusion, however, is not supported by the evidence on debt–equity ratios in the United States. Those ratios vary widely among industries, indicating that no single optimizing rule, such as "raise the debt–equity ratio as high as possible," holds.[4]

One of the reasons for the unrealistic conclusion reached by Modigliani and Miller is their oversimplified description of the U.S. tax system. In particular, they did not take into account the preferential tax treatment of personal capital gains. Along with others, Mervyn King and Joseph Stiglitz used a more complete and realistic description

---

[3] Modigliani and Miller, "The Cost of Capital," pp. 293-96.

[4] Ibid., pp. 282-84. Indeed, the statistical evidence presented by Modigliani and Miller, in which taxes were not properly treated, suggests that such a simple rule does not apply.

of the U.S. tax system in their analyses of optimal financial policy.[5] King compared the effects of financing new investment through issuing new shares, through retentions, and through issuing new debt on the value of equity in the firm. He found that, in the absence of any possibility of bankruptcy, maximization of the value of equity requires that new shares never be issued to finance investment.

Whether retentions or debt should be used, however, depends upon the various tax rates. Let m be the personal income tax rate, τ the corporation income tax rate, and z the effective personal income tax on capital gains; King shows that the firm will then finance new investment by means of retentions if

$$(4.1) \qquad (1 - m) < (1 - z)(1 - \tau).$$

The term on the left of this inequality, $(1 - m)$, is the after-tax return to an investor from a dollar in interest paid. $(1 - z)(1 - \tau)$ is the after-tax return to an investor of a dollar in retentions. Thus, if the effective tax burden on a dollar of interest is greater than the tax burden on a dollar in retentions, the firm should rely on retentions instead of debt.[6] If

$$(1 - m) > (1 - z)(1 - \tau),$$

then the effective tax burden on a dollar of retentions is greater than that on a dollar of debt and, consequently, the firm finances new investment by issuing debt.[7]

It is now clear why, in the absence of bankruptcy, optimal policy requires that new shares never be issued. Suppose that inequality 4.1 holds and, thus, the firm prefers retentions to debt finance; is it possible that the firm will prefer new issues to retentions? If new investment funds are raised by issuing new stock instead of retaining available profits, then the profits that are not now retained must be

---

[5] Joseph Stiglitz, "Taxation, Corporate Financial Policy, and the Cost of Capital," *Journal of Public Economics*, vol. 2 (February 1973), pp. 1-34; Mervyn King, "Taxation and the Cost of Capital," *Review of Economic Studies*, vol. 41 (1974), pp. 21-35; and Mervyn King, *Public Policy and the Corporation* (London: Chapman and Hall, 1977).

[6] See King, *Public Policy and the Corporation*, pp. 92-100, for a rigorous demonstration of this result.

[7] Stiglitz's analysis of the all-debt case goes a bit further. Since he was considering a firm that was just beginning, his all-debt policy implied essentially that the firm would never become a corporation. See Stiglitz, "Taxation, Corporate Financial Policy," p. 19. Along the same lines, King showed that it would be advantageous to incorporate a business if retentions were preferred to debt—that is, if inequality 4.1 holds. See King, *Public Policy and the Corporation*, pp. 112-16.

paid out as dividends.[8] The net-of-all-tax return to the stockholder of a dollar in dividends is $(1 - m)(1 - \tau)$, while the after-tax return to the stockholder from retaining a dollar is $(1 - z)(1 - \tau)$. As long as there is preferential treatment of capital gains, m will be larger than z and the firm will always prefer financing through retentions rather than through new issues with the consequent increase in dividend payments.[9]

Thus, if the firm prefers retentions to debt, it will also prefer retentions to new issues. What if the tax rates are such that the firm prefers to finance investment by means of debt rather than retentions? Will it also prefer debt to new issues? Suppose that the firm decreases its issue of new debt in a given year and issues new stock instead. In ensuing years, there will be more equity profits because of the new stock. These additional equity profits will not be retained but will be paid out in dividends, for it has already been stated that the firm at least prefers using debt rather than retentions to finance new investment. As in the previous instance, issuing new stock increases dividend payments. But as long as there is a corporation income tax, the net return on a dollar of dividends, given by $(1 - m)(1 - \tau)$, is less than the net return on a dollar of interest, which is simply $(1 - m)$.

Clearly, then, analyses such as those of King and Stiglitz imply that firms never issue new stock and that the only choice in financing new investment is whether to use debt or retentions.[10] Further, since these analyses are based on a model of an economy in which the

---

[8] The fundamental equation for investment funding states that new funds must come from one of three sources: retentions, debt, or new issues. In this case, given the amount of investment funds needed and given that the firm prefers not to use debt, an increase in new issues implies a decrease in retentions of the amount of the new issues. This, in turn, implies an increase in dividends of that amount.

[9] Taken to its extreme, this argument implies that firms should never pay dividends. Retentions in excess of investment needs would be used to buy up outstanding stock, which in essence allows the investor to receive dividends taxed as capital gains. While there are legal constraints that prohibit a firm from regularly buying back a pro rata share of its stock from each of its stockholders in lieu of paying dividends, it is not clear why firms do not simply buy back shares on the open market. This has the effect of providing a capital gain rather than a dividend to all stockholders and consequently has a considerable tax advantage. One of the important subjects for future research is the development of a comprehensive theory of the reasons that firms pay dividends.

[10] Stiglitz went a bit further than this. He considered a firm just beginning and concluded that stock is *never* issued in return for investment funds. The only way in which stock values are created is through the capitalization of the value of an idea in the form of an issue of stock to the entrepreneur. See Stiglitz, "Taxation, Corporate Financial Policy," pp. 17-19.

Modigliani-Miller theorem holds, the results are extremely sensitive to the tax rate. In the absence of taxes, financial policy is irrelevant; if the tax burden on retentions is slightly less than that on debt, the firm will not borrow and will finance investment entirely from retentions. If the corporation income tax raises the tax burden on retentions slightly above that on debt, the firm will switch completely to borrowing for all investment funds. It should therefore be expected that firms will choose either very high or very low debt–equity ratios. Not all firms will follow the same policy, however, since with a progressive tax system the values of m and z vary from one investor to the next and, if the relevant values of these personal tax rates for a given firm are those of the "representative" stockholder or the median voting stockholder, some firms may choose to finance entirely through debt, others entirely through retentions.[11]

Actually, this conclusion is too strong. Stiglitz's analysis, which was of a corporation in the process of formation, in operation for a number of years, then ceasing operations, stressed that a firm which wishes to finance entirely through retentions, particularly if it is newly formed, may not have a sufficiently high level of profits to finance its desired investment policy. In such an instance, the firm will retain all profits and borrow the extra funds necessary to finance its investment plans.[12] Later in the life of the firm, when profits exceed investment needs, the excess profits will be used to retire debt. Thus firms, particularly in their early stages, may follow an intermediate financial policy.

Even when the results are modified to take into account the life cycle of a firm, the King-Stiglitz type of analysis does not give, and is not really intended to give, an accurate picture of the behavior of corporations operating in the United States today. In particular, the wide diversity of financial policies followed by modern corporations suggests, though it does not prove, that the simple and very strong rules concerning optimal policy derived by King, Stiglitz, and others are not followed by corporations.[13] Further, the strongest conclusion of

---

[11] As firms will tend to specialize, so will investors. Those whose incomes are high will prefer stock in order to take advantage of the preferential treatment of capital gains, while those whose incomes are low will prefer debt.

[12] See Stiglitz, "Taxation, Corporate Financial Policy," p. 18. While King usually implicitly assumes that retentions are sufficient to finance investment plans, he does recognize that if they are not, the firm should borrow the extra funds. King, *Public Policy and the Corporation*, p. 95.

[13] See, for example, Eli Schwartz and J. Richard Aronson, "Some Surrogate Evidence in Support of the Concept of Optimal Financial Structure," *Journal of Finance*, vol. 22 (March 1967), pp. 10-18.

the King-Stiglitz analysis—that firms will never issue new stock—is also not consistent with experience in the United States. While issues of new stock are a smaller source of investment funds than issues of new debt and retentions, they are not negligible. In 1974, 1975, and 1976, new issues constituted 9.6 percent, 13.6 percent, and 13.0 percent of total new financing, respectively.[14] During those same years, new issues constituted about 20 percent of new equity financing.[15] Given that the costs of transactions associated with new issues are rather high, it might be expected that even without a corporation income tax new issues would make up a relatively small fraction of new finance. Consequently, the figures just given do not lend support to the conclusion that as a result of tax considerations no new stock will be issued.

The argument that the type of analysis made by King and Stiglitz is unrealistic is not really a criticism of such work. The assumptions of Modigliani and Miller upon which that analysis is based represent a kind of "pure case," the understanding of which is necessary as a beginning to an understanding of situations in the real world. Stiglitz likens his analysis to the study of a frictionless surface.[16] An understanding of the physics of motion is built upon the study of frictionless surfaces, but, for most practical problems, friction must be taken into account.[17] A thorough and rigorous theory of corporate financial policy in the presence of the many important frictions that exist in the U.S. economy has not yet been developed and is a formidable task for the future. Efforts have been made, however, to explore

---

[14] These figures are from the December 1977 issue of the *Federal Reserve Bulletin*. The corresponding figures for new issues less retirement of shares as a fraction of net new financing—that is, new financing less retirement of shares and debt—are 5.9 percent, 12.5 percent, and 11.4 percent, respectively.

[15] During that period, 41 percent of after-tax corporate profits net of the corporate tax were paid out as dividends so that, at least in the aggregate, profits were available that could have been retained in order to avoid new issues.

[16] Joseph Stiglitz, "On the Irrelevance of Corporate Financial Policy," *American Economic Review*, vol. 64 (December 1974), p. 866.

[17] One of the principal contributions of the work by King and Stiglitz is their demonstration that many of the preconceptions as to the effects of the corporation income tax are inconsistent with the simple, and idealized, models of behavior that many authors, not just King and Stiglitz, use. That work has shown that a thorough understanding of many institutional aspects of the U.S. economy and its tax structure is an integral part of a careful analysis of the effects of specific taxes. A good example of the importance of such analysis is King's book, *Public Policy and the Corporation*. In the early chapters King rigorously examines the effects of taxes in an idealized world; then he allows for realistic constraints on decision making by firms, ending with an empirical analysis that will be discussed below.

various aspects of corporate financial policy and taxation in realistic settings.

Many authors have argued that the single most important and unrealistic assumption of the Modigliani-Miller world is the assumption that bankruptcy is impossible or that, if it is possible, all investors agree on the probability that bankruptcy will occur.[18] Stiglitz concluded that if bankruptcy is possible and if different investors have different expectations, "the tax advantages of debt would increase the debt–equity ratio from what it would have been otherwise, but would not result in the firm going to an all debt position."[19] In keeping with the idealized world of the Modigliani-Miller model, much of the analysis of bankruptcy in that world uses the assumption that there are no costs associated with bankruptcy.[20] If that is the case, the assumption that investors differ in their expectations is crucial for the result just quoted. What limits the willingness of the owners of the firm to borrow in the presence of the tax advantages of debt is the fact that potential lenders may have a greater expectation of bankruptcy than the owners and, thus, may require a higher risk premium than the owners are willing to pay. Consequently, the owners will prefer to offer such potential lenders equity rather than debt. Unfortunately, rigorous analysis of this situation becomes extremely complex, because if investors differ in their expectations they will also differ in their views of what constitutes the optimal policy of the

---

[18] See, for example, Vernon Smith, "Default Risk, Scale and the Homemade Leverage Theorem," *American Economic Review*, vol. 62 (March 1972); David Baron, "Default Risk, Homemade Leverage and the Modigliani-Miller Theorem," *American Economic Review*, vol. 64 (March 1974), pp. 176-82; and Joseph Stiglitz, "Some Aspects of the Pure Theory of Corporation Finance, Bankruptcy and Takeover," *Bell Journal of Economics and Management Science*, vol. 3 (1972), pp. 458-83.

[19] Stiglitz, "Taxation, Corporate Financial Policy," p. 23. An implicit assumption of Stiglitz's analysis is that complete markets do not exist for all contingent commodities. A contingent commodity is a commodity to be delivered contingent upon some state of the world—an umbrella to be delivered next week if it is raining, for example. The existence of complete markets for all contingent commodities implies that there are separate markets for each commodity for each different possible state of the world. Continuing with the example of the umbrella, the existence of complete markets requires that there be one market for umbrellas to be delivered next week if it rains and a separate market for umbrellas to be delivered next week if it does not rain. Given the virtually infinite number of possible future states of the world, the assumption that complete markets do not exist for all contingent commodities seems reasonable.

[20] The assumption that bankruptcy imposes no cost means essentially that upon going into bankruptcy a firm is not liquidated but is reorganized at no cost, with the holders of its debt becoming the owners of the firm.

firm. Maximization of share values may not be preferred by all or even a majority of shareholders.[21]

Recently several authors have allowed for not only the possibility of bankruptcy, but also for the fact that there are costs associated with bankruptcy.[22] If bankruptcy is costly, then there will be an optimal debt–equity ratio in the absence of taxes, even if all investors agree on the possibility of bankruptcy. Further, the corporation income tax will cause firms to increase their debt–equity ratio but not to use only debt at the margin. The reason is that an increase in the debt–equity ratio raises the probability of bankruptcy and the expectation of its associated expected costs. Firms will increase their ratios of debt to equity until the increases in the expected costs of bankruptcy that would be associated with a small increase in debt finance are just compensated for by the tax savings from additional debt.

While the essential point about the nature of the effect of the costs of bankruptcy on corporate financial policy is valid, it is not clear that the actual costs of bankruptcy are large enough to make them an important determinant of policy. As pointed out by Robert Haugen and Lemma Senebet, the analyses that are based on the existence of bankruptcy costs take bankruptcy to be equivalent to liquidation.[23] Though the liquidation of a firm may be very costly, bankruptcy involves only the transfer of ownership to debtholders. That transfer may not be costly.[24]

For reasons other than the costs associated with bankruptcy, but related to the problem of bankruptcy, Stewart Myers has argued that under certain circumstances, and in the absence of taxes, firms will never issue risky debt.[25] His argument rests on the fact that part of the value of a firm is the present value of options for making favorable investments in the future. If the firm issues risky debt, it commits itself to future payments of interest that may not be covered by profits

---

[21] This point is discussed by a number of authors. See, for example, King, *Public Policy and the Corporation*, pp. 126-65, and the references in footnote 18 above.

[22] See, for example, James H. Scott, Jr., "The Theory of Optimal Capital Structure," *Bell Journal of Economics*, vol. 7 (Spring 1975), pp. 33-54.

[23] Robert A. Haugen and Lemma W. Senebet, "The Insignificance of Bankruptcy Costs to the Theory of Optimal Capital Structure," *Journal of Finance*, vol. 33 (May 1978), pp. 383-94. See also J. B. Warner, "Bankruptcy Costs, Absolute Priority and the Pricing of Risky Debt Claims," *Journal of Financial Economics*, vol. 4 (1977), pp. 239-76.

[24] Note that the costs of bankruptcy must not be confused with the operating costs that lead to bankruptcy.

[25] Stewart C. Myers, "Determinants of Corporate Borrowing," *Journal of Financial Economics*, vol. 5 (1977), pp. 147-75.

from the investment financed by the debt. Suppose that the firm is in fact committed to future interest payments not matched by the returns from a past investment. Then the firm may not accept some future investment if that investment cannot provide a fair return in addition to covering the interest commitments. In the absence of any interest commitments, the firm would accept such an investment if it provided a fair return. Since, as just mentioned, part of the value of the firm is the value of future investment options, and the presence of risky debt implies that in some future situations the firm will refuse what would otherwise be favorable investments, risky debt reduces the present value of the firm. Consequently, in the absence of taxes, firms should never issue risky debt. Myers also shows that a corporation income tax, by making even risky debt attractive for tax purposes, will induce the firm to issue some risky debt.[26]

Under the present tax system of the United States there are a number of other possible reasons for firms not to follow all-debt or all-retentions policies. Transactions costs associated with issuing debt may cause firms to rely at least partially on retentions instead of debt at the margin. Managers may prefer to follow stable dividend policies and to avoid high debt–equity ratios in order to protect their jobs.[27] Or, in a realistic setting, the various investors in a large corporation may have widely varying incomes and thus be subject to different rates of personal income tax. Management may need to attempt to balance the preferences of some stockholders for high debt–equity ratios against the preferences of others for low debt–equity ratios.[28]

So far we have stressed theoretical analyses of the effect of taxes on the financial policies of corporations. Not a great deal of econometric work has been done on this subject. What has been done, however, does suggest that the corporation income tax has caused corporations to rely more—but not entirely—on debt finance. Luigi Tambini used the results of some work by Fisher and Kolin who estimated the impact an increase in the debt–equity ratio has on risk

---

[26] Myers deals with taxes and their influence in the appendix to "Determinants of Corporate Borrowing," pp. 172-74.

[27] See, for example, Gordon Donaldson, "Financial Goals: Management vs. Stockholders," *Harvard Business Review*, vol. 41 (1963), pp. 116-29, or Li Way Lee, "A Theory of Management and Its Implications for Capital Structure and Merger," *Southern Economic Journal*, vol. 46 (July 1979), pp. 107-18.

[28] King has provided a rough sketch of a model in which management tries to accommodate conflicting preferences of stockholders as well as to avoid possible takeovers by other firms. See King, *Public Policy and the Corporation*, pp. 144-65.

premiums for debt and equity holders.[29] In Tambini's model, an increase in the corporation income tax rate increases the cost of equity funds and causes the firm to shift to a higher proportion of debt finance. This shift is limited by the rise in risk premiums on both debt and equity. Using the estimates of Lawrence Fisher and Marshall Kolin, Tambini calculated how much of a shift in the debt–equity ratio could be expected as a result of changes in the corporation income tax during the period 1927–1965; these calculations were then compared with the actual changes in the aggregate ratio of debt to equity in the manufacturing industry during that period. Tambini consistently found that the actual changes in debt–equity ratios were as he predicted them to be from his model. While it must be recognized that Tambini's model of optimal financial policy is much less thorough and less sophisticated than the analyses discussed earlier, his empirical work nevertheless provides strong evidence that the corporation income tax has increased debt–equity ratios but has not brought about complete reliance on debt or retentions at the margin.

Recognizing the complexity of optimal financial policy in the presence of the possibility of bankruptcy, differing expectations, costs associated with bankruptcy, the possibility of a firm's being taken over by another firm, investors subject to different tax rates, and similar "frictions," King provides an empirical analysis of the determinants of debt–equity ratios that is not explicitly based on the optimizing behavior which he examined rigorously and which was discussed above. Instead, his empirical analysis involves "estimating simple relationships which emphasize the effect of taxation."[30] Specifically, he hypothesizes that the desired ratio of debt to equity is positively related to the tax advantage of debt over new issues and the tax advantage of debt over retentions. He finds that the latter tax advantage is insignificant but that the former is an important determinant of debt–equity ratios. Indeed, when King includes a variable to measure the level of corporate takeovers in the economy, the simple estimating equation using that variable and the tax advantage of debt over new issues explains more than 80 percent of the variation in the aggregate debt–equity ratio of industrial and commercial companies in the United Kingdom during the period 1955–1971.[31]

[29] Luigi Tambini, "Financial Policy and the Corporation Income Tax," in *The Taxation of Income From Capital*, ed. Arnold Harberger and Martin J. Bailey (Washington, D.C.: The Brookings Institution, 1969), pp. 185-222.

[30] King, *Public Policy and the Corporation*, pp. 222-23.

[31] The reasoning behind the inclusion of the level of corporate takeovers is as follows: any given firm will think it more likely that an attempt to acquire it will be made if a large number of other firms have recently been taken over

What evidence there is, then, is consistent with the view that the corporation income tax and the capital gains tax are important determinants of financial policy.[32] The evidence is still sketchy, however, and it is important that more work, particularly empirical work, be done in order to arrive at a clearer understanding of the relationships between taxes and corporate financial policy.

Up to this point we have treated the dividend policy of a firm only peripherally. Since the decision to pay dividends is also a decision not to retain more earnings, dividend policy cannot really be separated from the decision whether to use debt or equity to finance new investments. It will be useful, however, to consider the determinants of dividend policy briefly by themselves. As might be expected, analysis based on the assumptions of Modigliani and Miller gives strong conclusions about this issue. In particular, Stiglitz concludes that firms should never pay dividends.[33] However, there has been some empirical work based on a rather ad hoc, but fairly plausible, model of dividend behavior which gives more realistic conclusions than those of Stiglitz.

Feldstein, King, and Brittain have used such a model to test the hypothesis that the dividend–payout ratio (the fraction of after-tax equity profits paid out as dividends) is a function of the cost of paying $1.00 in dividends net of all taxes in terms of retentions forgone net of all taxes.[34] In the United States this relative cost is determined by the preferential treatment of capital gains and by the delay in taxing retentions until stock has been sold and the retentions have been realized as capital gains. For example, a U.S. corporation may earn $4.00 in equity income and pay, let us say, a 50 percent corporate income tax, leaving $2.00 for stockholders. Suppose that the personal income of stockholders is taxed at a marginal rate of 50 percent. Then,

---

successfully. In order to reduce the possibility of being taken over, a firm will reduce its reliance upon debt. For if a firm relies heavily on debt, then it is easier for some group to purchase the relatively small amount of equity necessary to take it over. (A firm has been taken over when outsiders purchase enough stock to gain voting control of it.) If the firm relies heavily on equity, then a much larger expenditure will be necessary. Consequently, King argues that debt–equity ratios will decline as corporate acquisitions increase.

[32] See also Yoram C. Peles and Marshall Sarnat, "Corporate Taxes and Capital Structure: Some Evidence Drawn from the British Experience," *Review of Economics and Statistics*, vol. 61 (February 1979), pp. 118-20.

[33] Stiglitz, "Taxation, Corporate Financial Policy," pp. 17-20.

[34] See John A. Brittain, "The Tax Structure and Corporate Dividend Policy," *American Economic Review*, vol. 54 (May 1964); Martin S. Feldstein, "Corporate Taxation and Dividend Behavior," *Review of Economic Studies*, vol. 37 (1970); and Mervyn King, *Public Policy and the Corporation*, pp. 166-203.

if the $2.00 is paid in dividends, stockholders will keep $1.00 after payment of personal taxes. If, however, the $2.00 is retained, stockholders will pay no current tax, though when the stock is sold they will pay a capital gains tax on the $2.00. Bailey has estimated the present value of the effective personal tax rate on retentions to be about 8 percent.[35] Thus, if the $2.00 is retained, stockholders receive $1.84 in after-tax retentions. Accordingly, $1.00 in dividends costs $1.84 in retentions forgone. Using data from the United Kingdom, Feldstein and King both found that such a cost of dividends in relation to retentions is a significant determinant of firms' dividend–payout ratios.

In comparison with the empirical analysis of the determinants of firms' debt–equity ratios, the empirical analyses of taxes and dividend–payout ratios by King and Feldstein are thorough and convincing. However, David Bradford has recently presented a strikingly simple argument which implies that the tax cost of dividends in relation to the tax cost of retentions has no effect on the dividend–payout ratio of a firm.[36] Bradford shows that in an economy in which the assumptions of Modigliani and Miller prevail—in which without taxes the debt–equity ratio and dividend–payout ratio of a firm are irrelevant— a tax that is imposed on all dividends in the absence of other taxes does not alter the dividend–payout ratio.[37] This is true in spite of the fact that such a tax increases the cost of dividends in relation to retentions and, according to the empirical analyses of Feldstein and King, would reduce the dividend–payout ratio significantly.

Bradford's rigorous analysis of this issue is quite complex, but he provides a simple intuitive explanation of his conclusion, as follows: Consider the tax on dividends as analogous to a tax on withdrawals from savings accounts opened before the imposition of the tax. Suppose that before the tax a person had $100.00 in such an account and that, without warning, a 50 percent tax was imposed on withdrawals. That person could sell the rights to withdraw from his

---

[35] Martin J. Bailey, "Capital Gains and Income Taxation," in *The Taxation of Income from Capital*, ed. by Arnold C. Harberger and Martin J. Bailey (Washington, D.C.: The Brookings Institution, 1969), pp. 11-49. Changes that have since been made in the capital gains tax laws have put this figure out of date. It should be considered only a rough estimate of the effective tax rate.

[36] David F. Bradford, "The Incidence and Allocation Effects of a Tax on Corporate Distributions," 1977, processed.

[37] Bradford's analysis has been extended to the case in which there are both a corporation income tax and a personal income tax, as in the United States, by Alan J. Auerbach, in "Wealth Maximization and the Cost of Capital," National Bureau of Economic Research working paper no. 254 (1978). He confirms Bradford's results under such a tax system.

account for only $50.00. He would have no incentive, however, to alter the timing of his withdrawals from that account. Any holder of such an account would suffer a capital loss, but he could not regain any of that loss by retaining more of the interest payments on his investment rather than withdrawing them or withdrawing the principal.

With respect to corporate equity, Bradford's point is that a tax on dividends imposes a capital loss on stockholders which does not alter the pattern of dividend payments. Bradford's analysis, however, like that of Stiglitz and King, implies that there is no optimal debt–equity ratio in the absence of taxes, that once the tax has been imposed new stock is never issued, and that, in the absence of taxes, the optimal dividend–payout ratio is indeterminate. It must be understood, therefore, that Bradford's analysis is of an idealized, unrealistic economy. Nonetheless, that analysis makes it clear that the simple hypotheses of the effect of taxes on dividend policy underlying the empirical analyses of King and Feldstein must be expanded upon before final conclusions as to the actual effect of taxes on dividends can be reached. Stiglitz has recently argued that a more thorough theory of dividend policy must be based on an idea that has been discussed for some time, namely, that dividends provide an important signaling service to investors.[38] Since shareholders and potential shareholders do not have complete information about the profit-making prospects of a firm— information that will aid them in making up their portfolios—the level and the long-term trend of the dividends paid by a firm may provide some of the information that they desire. While dividends are not a perfect source of information—and could even be used by management to misinform investors—they are a potential source of information, the value of which may be weighed against the cost of the double taxation of dividends.

The Cost of Capital, Financial Policy, and the Corporation Income Tax

As mentioned at the beginning of this chapter, many of the economic effects discussed in Chapters 2 and 3 arise from the fact that a tax on the return to capital increases the cost of capital to a firm. Given the preceding discussion of optimal financial policy, we can now turn to the question of whether or not a tax on equity finance—one method of financing the capital stock of a firm—increases the cost of capital to the firm. If it does, many of the findings of Chapters 2 and 3 apply to a corporation income tax, though there must be some modifications; if it does not, then an entirely different view of the incidence of the

---

[38] Stiglitz, "On the Irrelevance of Corporate Financial Policy," p. 863, note 15. See also King, *Public Policy and the Corporation*, pp. 172–76.

corporation income tax and its effects on growth and efficiency is applicable.

The effect of the corporation income tax on the cost of capital is influenced by the tax treatment of depreciation as well as by the financial policies of the firm. Before considering the influence of financial policies, it will be useful to see why depreciation rules are important. Suppose that interest payments are not deductible under the corporation income tax and that firms are allowed immediate write-off of investment expenditures against current earnings.[39] Since both debt and equity are taxed, there is then no reason for the firm to adjust its debt–equity ratio when a corporation income tax is imposed. However, with immediate write-off of investment expenditures, the tax does not affect the cost of capital. Any investment project that was worth pursuing before the tax was imposed is worth pursuing after the tax has been imposed. To see this, suppose that the returns from an investment in each year are R_t (with both debt and equity taxed, it does not matter whether R is the return to holders of equity or to holders of debt), i is the discount rate, and the cost of the project is C. In the absence of the corporation tax, the investment will be undertaken if

$$\sum_{t=0}^{\infty} \frac{R_t}{(1+i)^t} > C.$$

When the tax has been imposed, the net returns become $R_t(1 - \tau)$, where τ is the corporation tax rate. But, with immediate write-off of investment costs, the net cost to the firm of the investment becomes $C(1 - \tau)$. Thus, after the tax has been imposed, the investment will be undertaken if

$$\sum_{t=0}^{\infty} \frac{R_t(1 - \tau)}{(1+i)^t} > C(1 - \tau),$$

which is the same as the condition given above.

In this case, all that the tax does is to cause the government to share equally in the cost and the returns from investment projects. This has no effect on the level of investment and, consequently, has no effect on the marginal productivity of new investment. As a result, the cost of capital, which is essentially the discount rate and is determined by the marginal productivity of new investment, will not be changed.[40]

---

[39] If current earnings are insufficient, then the firm is guaranteed the present value of this write-off at some future time.

[40] We are abstracting from the effects of changes in income and wealth on the willingness of individuals to save.

Without immediate write-off of investment expenditures, the financial policies of a firm and the tax deductibility of interest payments become important in determining the effect of tax changes on the cost of capital. Let r be the rate of return on an investment project before tax but after depreciation. Then an investment will be undertaken if

$$(4.2) \qquad r > \frac{\alpha \, r_e}{(1 - t_e)} + \frac{(1 - \alpha)i}{1 - m} + (1 - \lambda)\frac{\delta}{(1 - \tau_e)},$$

where α is the proportion of the investment financed by equity, r_e is the net of all taxes rate of return required by equity holders to induce them to invest in the firm, t_e is the effective tax on equity, i is the rate of interest on corporate debt after personal income tax, λ is the proportion of depreciation expenses that are tax deductible, δ is the rate of depreciation, and, as before, τ is the corporation income tax rate and m is the personal tax rate. Clearly, if the firm is allowed to write off its true depreciation completely—that is, $\lambda = 1$—and the firm finances its marginal investments entirely through the use of debt—that is, $\alpha = 0$—then r, the required return on new investments, which is also the cost of capital to the firm, is independent of the corporation income tax rate. The cost of capital to the firm is simply the interest rate.

Recall that King's analysis—and for that matter, Stiglitz's—implies that the firm will rely entirely on debt finance if $(1 - m) > (1 - z)(1 - r)$. The reason that the financial policy of the firm in this case is so important to the issue of the incidence of the corporation income tax now becomes clear. If the firm relies entirely on debt at the margin, then the corporation income tax does not increase the cost of capital to corporations, the investment plans of corporations do not change, there is no flow of capital from the corporate sector to the noncorporate sector, the normal rate of return to capital does not decline, and, apart from wealth effects on savings, there is no change in the equilibrium growth path of the economy—that is, the principal adjustments to the tax discussed in Chapter 3, where it was indicated that the tax burden is diffused to all agents in the economy, do not occur. Those who own stock at the time of the imposition of the tax bear the full burden of the tax in the form of a capital loss. Since new stock is never issued and all further investment relies on debt, no one else bears any tax burden.

If the firm relies on retentions instead of debt, then in the ideal world assumed by King and Stiglitz it must be that the cost of debt is greater than the cost of equity. This implies that with true depreciation allowed, $r_e/(1 - t_e) < i/(1 - m)$. But, if the firm can always invest at the market rate of interest—that is, if it can use its investment funds to buy financial securities—then the firm will never use retentions to pursue projects whose return is less than the interest rate, $i/(1 - m)$. Consequently, the firm will pursue all projects whose expected return is greater than the interest rate and, if any retentions are left over, it will buy financial securities that pay the market rate of interest. Thus the marginal return to capital in the corporate sector—the corporate cost of capital—is again the interest rate. And, as before, an increase in the corporation income tax does not increase the cost of capital and has none of the effects discussed in the previous chapter. Further, since excess retentions are used to buy financial assets, dividends are never paid, and t_e is the corporate tax rate plus the present value of the preferential personal tax rate on retentions.

There are other cases that can be discussed within the context of the idealized models of King and Stiglitz—that of the firm which prefers retentions, for example, but is legally constrained from purchasing financial securities; however, we shall turn instead to a more realistic setting in which the firm uses both debt and equity finance, pays dividends, and retains earnings. Clearly, if the firm uses both debt and equity, the cost of capital, r in inequality 4.2, will be increased by the corporation income tax. Further, if firms pay dividends, the tax rate on equity, t_e, will be a weighted average of the tax on retentions and the double tax on dividends.

In some analyses a rather simple model of the determination of corporate financial policy has been used that is consistent with the thrust of those studies in which the addition of greater realism to the King-Stiglitz models has been attempted. This simple model of corporate financial policy requires the assumption that because of the risk of bankruptcy and the costs imposed by bankruptcy, a firm must increase the risk premium paid to its investors if it increases its debt–equity ratio. Faced with this fact and the tax advantages of debt, firms choose a debt–equity ratio that minimizes their cost of capital. In such a framework, an increase in the corporation income tax does increase the cost of capital to a firm; the firm is able to offset some of this increase, however, by switching to a higher debt–equity ratio. As will be discussed below, if this is an accurate description of corporate financial policy, then it is likely that the burden of the corporation income tax will be diffused throughout the economy.

Ballentine and McLure add just such a simple model of financial policy to the static two-sector Harberger model of tax incidence.[41]

---

[41] J. Gregory Ballentine and Charles E. McLure, Jr., "Taxation and Corporate Financial Policy," *Quarterly Journal of Economics* (forthcoming).

Their model includes three assets—corporate debt, corporate equity, and noncorporate capital. The risk premiums on corporate debt and equity are expressed as a markup over the after-tax return available in the noncorporate sector. Writing the after-tax return in the noncorporate sector as i_n, this version of the simple model of financial policy assumes that r_e/i_n and i/i_n both increase with any increase in the debt–equity ratio of the firm.[42]

With this brief sketch of their model, the main conclusions of Ballentine and McLure's analysis can be easily understood. Each corporation chooses an optimal debt–equity ratio that just balances the tax advantages of debt against the increased risk premiums resulting from debt finance. An increase in the corporation income tax causes the firm to switch more toward debt. That increase also raises the marginal cost of capital to corporations. The latter induces capital flows and changes in output that are the same as those of the traditional Harberger model discussed in Chapter 3. Indeed, Ballentine and McLure find that the total burden on capitalists as a group is almost exactly the same in their model as it is in the standard Harberger model.

It is in the distribution of the burden among capitalists that the Ballentine and McLure results are novel. The increase in the debt–equity ratios of corporations induced by an increase in the corporation income tax increases the returns on equity and on corporate debt relative to the return in the noncorporate sector—that is, i/i_n and r_e/i_n both increase. Consequently, though all capitalists suffer a decline in their rate of return, those owning noncorporate capital bear the greatest burden. This is in contrast to the traditional result obtained by using the Harberger model, wherein no distinction is made between debt and equity finance, it is assumed that rates of return are equalized between sectors, and the conclusion is thus reached that all capitalists share the burden of the tax equally. The Ballentine-McLure result, which they refer to as an overshifting of the tax to the noncorporate sector, implies that the incidence of the tax is less progressive than it appears to be from the Harberger results. This is because noncorporate capitalists, who are largely owners of housing and real estate, tend to have lower incomes than those whose principal assets are corporate securities.

As Ballentine and McLure stress in their paper, these results must be viewed cautiously. Part of the increase in both corporate returns

---

[42] Note that expressing the risk premiums as a markup over the noncorporate return does not imply that noncorporate investments are without risk but only that the risk in that sector does not change when the debt–equity ratio in the corporate sector changes.

relative to the noncorporate return is simply a compensation for the greater risk associated with the increased corporate debt–equity ratio. Marginal investors in the corporate sector will not benefit at all from the greater relative return. Inframarginal investors, however, who are less risk-averse than the marginal investor, will benefit from the greater relative returns. If, but for differences in income, individuals are similar in their attitudes toward risk and if they exhibit decreasing absolute risk aversion, then stockholders having large incomes will be less risk-averse than others and they will gain as risk premiums rise. How much they will gain requires a more complete modeling of preferences in the presence of risk than that given by Ballentine and McLure.

Martin Feldstein, Jerry Green, and Eytan Sheshinski also used a fairly simple model of financial policy to examine corporate taxation and financial policy in a growing economy.[43] In order to avoid any ambiguity involved in interpreting changes in rates of return, Feldstein, Green, and Sheshinski assumed that the debt–equity ratios of each firm and of the economy as a whole are constant. Consequently, risk taking does not change in their model, and any increase or decline in the rates of return on debt or equity implies a clear gain or loss to investors. While this simplifies interpretation of their results, that simplification is bought at a high price, for their assumption implies that firms do not alter their debt–equity ratios in response to changes in the tax on equity.

Even under their rigid assumption of constant debt–equity ratios, Feldstein, Green, and Sheshinski show that part of the burden of a tax on the income from equity capital is borne by those who own debt capital. Since their model does not include a noncorporate sector, the implication of this result is that a tax on the income from equity capital is borne at least partially by all capitalists. A detailed explanation of the reasons for the results obtained by Feldstein, Green, and Sheshinski is rather complex. It is sufficient to note here that their model shows that, since debt and equity are alternative methods of financing the same input (capital), a tax on one method of finance will have repercussions in all financial markets, thereby diffusing the tax burden throughout the economy.[44]

---

[43] Martin Feldstein, Jerry Green, and Eytan Sheshinski, "Corporate Financial Policy and Taxation in a Growing Economy," *Quarterly Journal of Economics* (forthcoming).

[44] In order to simplify their analysis, Feldstein, Green, and Sheshinski assumed that the aggregate rate of saving in the economy is fixed. From the discussion of taxation in growing economies given in Chapter 3, it is clear that if savings rates are positively related to the return on savings, then Feldstein, Green, and

Summary

It is difficult to provide a precise synthesis of the current discussion of corporate financial policy and the tax system of the United States. The analysis clearly indicates that under the idealizing assumptions of Modigliani and Miller the effect of the corporation income tax is not at all like the effect of the tax discussed in Chapters 2 and 3. In such a frictionless world the tax falls only on those who owned stock when the tax was imposed. It has no effect on the marginal cost of capital, the price of corporate output, the incomes of workers or holders of debt and noncorporate capital, the return on new investment, or the level of investment.[45]

In a more realistic setting, however, it appears likely that the burden of the tax is diffused much as discussed in Chapter 3. As long as firms are not indifferent to their debt–equity ratios in the absence of taxes—in particular, if firms must pay higher risk premiums to investors when they increase their debt–equity ratios—then the corporation income tax will increase the marginal cost of capital. That increase in the marginal cost of capital will set off a sequence of adjustments, including a flow of capital from corporate to noncorporate ventures, a decline in the interest rate earned on new savings—that is, on new investment—and an increase in the price of corporate output, which implies an increase in the price of new capital goods. Consequently, the burden of the tax is diffused among all capitalists and all consumers of corporate products, and in the long run, because of a decline in investment, the income of labor is also reduced by the tax.

Sheshinski's results imply that the tax will decrease savings. Consequently, the tax will decrease the capital–labor ratio in the economy, causing the tax burden to be borne partially by labor.

[45] This is a bit of an overstatement, since the stockholders who suffer a loss may alter their decisions to save and thus change investment in the economy. This is likely to have only a slight effect, however.

5

Capital Shortages and the Welfare Cost of the Corporation Income Tax

In the preceding chapters it has been argued that the gains in equity brought about by the use of the corporation income tax as a principal source of revenues are, at best, uncertain. Any rational society must ask at what costs in inefficiency and reduced growth those uncertain gains in equity are purchased. The answer to that question is not easily obtained; there is growing evidence, however, that the welfare cost of the corporation income tax is high.

Obviously, a large share of the cost imposed on the private economy by any tax is accounted for by the revenues that the tax transfers to the government. However, as is true of virtually all taxes, the corporation income tax imposes a burden in excess of the transfer to the government by inducing price distortions and inefficiencies in the economy. Indeed, as will be discussed in this chapter, this excess burden of the corporation income tax may amount to more than 50 percent of the revenues generated by that tax. Stated more simply, it may well be that for every dollar the government gains in revenues, the private economy loses $1.50 or more, which means that the net excess burden on the whole economy was about $30 billion in 1977.

The inefficiency of the corporation income tax arises from the fact that the tax induces a capital shortage in the corporate sector of the economy. That shortage is the result of both a misallocation of capital between the corporate and the noncorporate sectors and a suboptimal level of new corporate investment. In the next section we discuss the efficiency cost of the corporation income tax in a static economy with full factor mobility. It is in this context that the sectoral misallocation of capital caused by the tax is most easily highlighted. In the third section we take economic growth into account and stress the important effect of the tax on new investment.

In virtually all the literature in which the efficiency cost of the corporation income tax has been analyzed and an attempt to quantify it has been made, the basic approach discussed in Chapter 3 has been followed—that is, the tax has been treated as one that is assessed against the total return to capital in the corporate sector. As argued in the last section of the preceding chapter, this approach is basically sound as long as firms do not rely entirely on debt to finance new investment.[1] Throughout the bulk of this chapter we will follow the literature on the excess burden of corporate taxation—that is, we will assume that firms do not adjust their financial policies in response to changes in the tax, and thus we will treat the corporate tax as a tax on capital income in the corporate sector of the economy.

Capital Tax Differentials and the Misallocation of Capital

Using the same model that he developed for his study of the incidence of the corporation income tax, Harberger estimated the efficiency cost of that tax to be about 0.5 percent of national income.[2] This estimate actually pertains to the effect of equalizing the total tax rates on capital between a high-tax sector, the corporate sector, and a low-tax sector, the noncorporate sector. Given the size of the corporation income tax, abolishing that tax is an important aspect of such tax equalization. However, equalization also involves imposing appropriate personal taxes on retentions and equalizing sectoral property-tax differentials. Since such a policy change has been dealt with in virtually all the work on the static inefficiency of capital income taxes, the results discussed here have to do with the gains in welfare to be made from abolishing all sectoral differences in the tax rates on capital income. Toward the end of this section we will consider briefly the effect of reducing the corporation income tax alone.

While Harberger's two-sector model has been disaggregated in the most recent work on capital income tax differentials and his estimates have been improved, we will begin with a discussion of the welfare cost of differing sectoral taxes on capital using that two-sector

[1] Under the idealizing assumptions of Modigliani and Miller, the tax causes no efficiency loss. Recall, from the discussion of the analyses by King and Stiglitz, that in such an idealized world the tax has no effect in the economy except to impose a capital loss on those who own stock at the time at which the tax is imposed. Consequently, the tax does not increase the cost of capital to corporations and thus does not cause a misallocation of capital or a suboptimal level of new investment.

[2] Arnold C. Harberger, "Efficiency Effects of Taxes on Income from Capital," in *Effects of Corporation Income Tax*, ed. Marian Krzyzaniak (Detroit: Wayne State University Press, 1966), pp. 110-17.

model, because it is easiest to explain the nature of the welfare cost in a simple model. Then we will turn to the numerical estimates of excess burden generated by more complex large-scale models.

The corporation income tax is a factor market distortion. It increases corporations' marginal cost of capital to a level higher than that of noncorporate firms. This cost differential implies that capital and labor will be inefficiently allocated in such a way that the value of the marginal product of capital in the corporate sector will be higher than that in the noncorporate sector and the marginal rate of technical substitution of capital for labor will not be the same in all sectors. As demonstrated in the literature on factor market distortions, this inefficient allocation of resources will cause the economy to operate inside its production possibility frontier.[3] In Figure 3, let X be corporate output and Y be noncorporate output. Let the curve ONZ be the production possibility frontier of the economy; it shows the maximum combinations of the two outputs which can be produced given full employment and the present state of technology. If there are no factor market distortions, the fully employed economy will operate somewhere along the production-possibility curve. If there is a corporation income tax, however, the consequent inefficient allocation of capital and labor will cause even the fully employed economy to operate inside its production possibility curve somewhere along a line such as OCZ.

In addition to causing the economy to operate inside its production possibility frontier, the tax distorts the relative prices of outputs by artificially increasing the cost of corporate output. Consequently, the level of corporate and noncorporate output preferred by society, even along the inner curve OCZ, is distorted. By reacting to the distorted relative price line $P'P'$ in Figure 3, the economy ends up at a point such as A instead of the point C.[4] (II and $I'I'$ are two social indifference curves.) Clearly society has suffered a loss of welfare because of the fact that it operates along the inner curve OCZ and that along that inner curve the point A is chosen instead of C.

---

[3] See, for example, Ronald Jones, "Distortions in Factor Markets and the General Equilibrium Model of Production," *Journal of Political Economy*, vol. 79 (May/June, 1971), pp. 437-59.

[4] The slope of the line $P'P'$ is equal to the price of corporate output relative to the price of noncorporate output. At any point, the slope of the curve OCZ reflects the cost of extra corporate output in terms of noncorporate output forgone, given a constant corporate tax rate. That $P'P'$ cuts OCZ at point A—the after-tax equilibrium point—rather than being tangent to OCZ reflects the fact that the tax has caused the price of corporate output relative to the price of noncorporate output to be greater than the true social cost of corporate output in noncorporate output forgone.

FIGURE 3

Output Determination in an Economy Distorted by a Corporation Income Tax

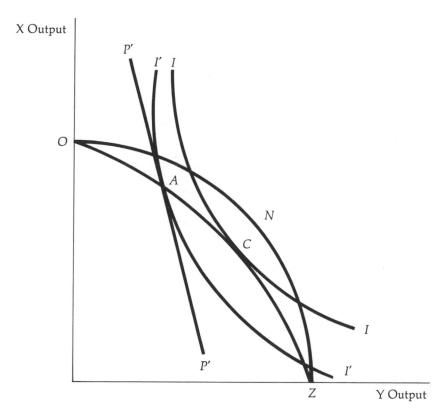

Figure 3 is a simple graphic representation of the waste caused by the corporation income tax in a static economy. The effect of the tax is basically the same as that of simply leaving some labor and capital idle and imposing an excise tax on corporate output. Given that the corporation income tax has this effect, it is obviously important to determine the value to society of the lost output. If P_x is the price of the corporate good and P_y is the price of the noncorporate good, then the value of the lost output is

(5.1)
$$P_x \Delta X + P_y \Delta Y,$$

where ΔX and ΔY are the changes in physical output of X and Y

induced by the tax.[5] As Harberger has shown, using the equations describing the production functions and profit maximization in his model, this formula for the welfare cost of the tax can be written as

$$(5.2) \qquad\qquad rt\Delta K_x,$$

where r is the after-tax return to capital, t is the corporation income tax rate expressed as a fraction of the net return, and ΔK_x is the decline in capital employed in the corporate sector because of the tax.[6]

An explanation of this formula is particularly useful for understanding the inefficiency of the corporation income tax. In maximizing their profits, both corporate and noncorporate firms employ capital to the point at which the value of the marginal product of capital is equal to the cost of capital. In the corporate sector the cost, and thus the value of the marginal product, of capital is $r(1+t)$, while in the noncorporate sector the cost and value of marginal product are simply r. Consider a small increase in the tax. As discussed in Chapter 3, this causes a flow of capital out of the corporate sector now denoted by ΔK_x. The value of the lost corporate output is the value of the marginal product of capital times the loss of capital—that is, $r(1+t)\Delta K_x$. Under full employment, the capital leaving the corporate sector is subsequently employed in the noncorporate sector, increasing the value of noncorporate output by $-r\Delta K_x$. (Since ΔK_x is negative, indicating an outflow of capital from the corporate sector, the resulting inflow of capital to the noncorporate sector is $-\Delta K_x$.) The net effect is a loss to society in the amount $rt\Delta K_x$.

The measure of welfare loss given in equation 5.2 is actually only accurate for a small change in the tax. In order to estimate the welfare loss that the entire extra tax on corporate income would cause, it is necessary to rely on an approximation of equation 5.2. Harberger uses the equations of his model to derive a linear approximation for ΔK_x; then using that linear approximation he estimates the entire welfare cost of the tax. The resulting estimates, referred to at the beginning of this section, suggest a loss of welfare equal to about 0.5 percent of national income.[7]

---

[5] This formula captures the loss of welfare arising from the fact that the economy is inside its production-possibility curve and the loss from the distortion in the relative prices of products. On this point, see Daniel M. Wisecarver, "The Social 'Costs of Input Market Distortions," *American Economic Review*, vol. 64 (June 1974), pp. 359-72. There is, however, an indeterminacy in this welfare-loss formula. P_x and P_y can represent prices either before or after the tax is changed. This indeterminacy gives rise to a kind of index-number problem that will be discussed briefly below.

[6] See Harberger, "Efficiency Effects of Taxes," pp. 108-10.

[7] Ibid., p. 116.

Shoven has used a twelve-sector model to refine Harberger's estimate.[8] Rather than rely on linear approximations, he calculates exact Paasche and Laspeyres indices of the loss in real national income resulting from the tax. That is, he calculates equation 5.1, first using before-tax values of P_x and P_y, then using the after-tax values. The first calculation is the Paasche index of the loss in real income, the second the Laspeyres index. It can be shown that the true value of the welfare loss lies between the Paasche and Laspeyres measures. In spite of his use of a disaggregated model and his correction of some numerical errors in Harberger's data, Shoven still found that the loss of welfare was equal to about 0.5 percent of national income.[9] It should be noted that this figure of 0.5 percent is likely to be an overstatement of the static welfare loss in the present-day economy, because it is derived using data on the U.S. economy during the years 1953–1957. During that period, corporate tax revenues were equal to a larger share of GNP than they are today. As Shoven pointed out, his estimate implies a loss of about 12 percent of the revenues derived from the tax. If the 12 percent figure is applied to the present level of corporate revenues, the result is a static welfare loss equal to about 0.3 percent of GNP.

While correcting for the fact that corporate tax revenues are equal to a smaller share of GNP today than in the 1950s decreases the estimates of the static welfare loss, further disaggregation is likely to increase them. As part of the continuing project mentioned in Chapter 3, Fullerton, King, Shoven, and Whalley have investigated the gains in welfare to be made by equalizing the tax rates on capital in all nineteen sectors of their model.[10] They estimate a welfare gain equal to almost 0.7 percent of GNP. In view of the level of disaggregation in their model and the richness of their description of the U.S. tax system, it is particularly important to recognize that this figure is an overstatement of the gains to be made by simply abolishing the corporation income tax. A closer estimate of the cost of the corporate tax would be their calculation of the gains to be made by abolishing the corporate income tax and taxing retentions as personal

---

[8] John B. Shoven, "The Incidence and Efficiency Effects of Taxes," pp. 1261-84.

[9] Ibid. Shoven showed that when Harberger's estimates are corrected for two numerical errors, the estimate of the loss of welfare declines to 0.3 percent of GNP. Upon disaggregation to twelve sectors, however, the estimate rises to 0.5 percent.

[10] Don Fullerton, Thomas King, John Shoven, and John Whalley, "A General Equilibrium Appraisal of U.S. Corporate and Personal Tax Integration," paper presented at the North American Meetings of the Econometric Society, New York, December 28, 1977.

income without equalizing the differentials in property taxes and other capital taxes. They find that such a tax change would produce a gain in welfare on the order of 0.4 percent of GNP.

While the estimates of the welfare cost of the corporation income tax appear to be fairly insensitive to the level of aggregation, other factors may cause those results to change significantly. In some preliminary work using a static, open-economy model in which four trading blocs—the United States, the European Economic Community, Japan, and the rest of the world—are incorporated, Whalley showed that the corporation income tax may actually provide a welfare gain for the United States.[11] Whalley assumed that each of the four trading blocs had a monopoly in the production of the goods that it exported. The firms in each country are assumed to be perfect competitors, however. As a consequence, the trading blocs do not exploit their monopoly power in world trade. In the United States the capital tax burden on manufactured exports is particularly high because of the corporation income tax. One of the effects of that high tax burden is an increase in the price of those exports. This means that the corporation income tax acts partially as an optimum tariff, allowing the United States to exploit its monopoly power in world trade. According to Whalley's preliminary numerical results, the advantage of the corporation income tax that is attributable to its effect of increasing export prices outweighs the losses attributable to the distortion in the capital market. As a result, removing the tax causes a loss in welfare.

This result should not be emphasized without further investigation. Whalley's conclusion was influenced significantly by two assumptions—first, that the United States has significant monopoly power in foreign trade, and second, that U.S. firms do not exploit any of that power. If the United States has little monopoly power, then the terms of trade will be virtually fixed and the corporation income tax will have few advantages in foreign trade. Even if the United States has

---

[11] John Whalley, "Discriminatory Features of Domestic Taxation Policies and Their Impact on World Trade: A General Equilibrium Approach," paper presented at the North American Meetings of the Econometric Society, Chicago, August 31, 1978. In Whalley's analysis, international movements of physical capital are ignored, as they have been throughout this study. Accurate modeling of such capital flows is a difficult task which must await further research. Whalley's basic model, however, does provide an excellent framework within which efforts can be made in the future to incorporate this potentially important aspect of corporate taxation. Whalley has already made a start in this effort by specifying in his model that investors in one country may own capital in other countries, though they cannot transfer that capital from one country to another.

monopoly power in its export markets, if U.S. firms are aware of that advantage and exploit it, there will be no further advantages in trade to be exploited through corporate taxes. Indeed, the corporate tax will be a disadvantage in foreign trade.

In a closed economy, the issue of corporate monopoly power also has some bearing on the efficiency cost of the corporation income tax. If corporations have and exploit some monopoly power, then even in the absence of corporate taxes the economy will be inefficient. The exercise of monopoly power by corporations induces a distortion of the product market—that is, corporations will charge a price that is in excess of their marginal cost, and their output will be reduced below the socially optimal level. In this case, a corporation income tax will not only induce a distortion in the factor market but will also aggravate the distortion in the product market by reducing corporate output further below the monopoly-restricted level. Estimates based on a simple, two-sector model in which corporations are imperfect competitors indicate that the aggravation of the distortion in the product market increases the efficiency cost of the corporation income tax about 25 percent.[12]

The importance of unexploited monopoly power in foreign trade or exploited monopoly power in domestic trade for analysis of the efficiency cost of the corporation income tax is indicative of the potential importance to this issue of a large number of distortions, some from taxes, some from other causes. The general literature on the theory of second best has shown that imposition of a single distortion in the presence of other distortions may have effects significantly different from the effects of imposing that distortion in a situation in which there are no other distortions. A good deal of work remains to be done in evaluation of the efficiency cost of the corporation income tax in a realistic setting in which there are pre-existing distortions, such as personal income taxes that distort choices between labor and leisure, regulated industries, and sectoral distortions in the labor market caused by union-maintained wage differentials.[13]

---

[12] See Anderson and Ballentine, "The Incidence and Excess Burden of a Profits Tax under Imperfect Competition."

[13] Johnson and Mieszkowski divided the economy into a union sector and a nonunion sector and estimated the welfare cost of a 15 percent markup of wages in the union sector over wages in the nonunion sector. Harry Johnson and Peter Mieszkowski, "The Effects of Unionization on the Distribution of Income: A General Equilibrium Approach," *Quarterly Journal of Economics*, vol. 84 (November 1970), pp. 539-61. Interestingly enough, their data show that the union sector pays higher taxes on capital than does the nonunion sector, indicating that the union sector is more heavily incorporated than the nonunion sector. This conclusion suggests that it would be worthwhile to investigate the

The first of these distortions may be particularly important if personal income taxes are increased to make up for revenues lost through abolition of the corporation income tax. An increase in personal income taxes will impose an efficiency cost by further distorting choices between labor and leisure, and that cost will at least partially offset the gain in efficiency from doing away with the corporation income tax.[14]

The estimates of potential gains in efficiency that have been discussed refer to the gains to be derived from equalizing the rates at which capital is taxed throughout the economy. A significant step could be taken in that direction by lowering or abolishing the corporation income tax, and the estimates discussed here are frequently taken as representing the magnitude of the efficiency cost of the corporation income tax. However, there is an important difference between equalizing the rates at which all sectoral capital income is taxed and removing the corporation income tax. If the corporation income tax is abolished and no personal tax is assessed against retained earnings, then the effective tax on corporate capital income will be less than that on noncorporate capital income—that is, an inefficient subsidy would exist that would produce the opposite of the effects discussed in this section. In particular, there would be a shortage of capital in the noncorporate sector. In a sense, simply abolishing the corporation income tax would go too far; the optimal policy would involve integrating corporate and personal income taxes so that effectively there would be no separate corporate income tax, and retentions would be taxed as personal income.

Some form of dividends-only integration—that is, the removal of a separate corporate tax on dividends while such a tax on retentions is retained—may be a more likely possibility than full integration. Since dividends-only integration reduces the tax on distributed corporate capital income but retains a tax on retentions, such a policy may well provide a greater gain in efficiency than would be achieved by abolishing the corporation income tax entirely.

---

loss of welfare attributable to the corporate income tax in a situation in which corporations must pay higher wages than unincorporated enterprises because of unionization.

[14] As will be discussed in the following section, Fullerton, Shoven, and Whalley have investigated just such an issue using a preliminary dynamic version of their nineteen-sector model. Don Fullerton, John Shoven, and John Whalley, "General Equilibrium Aspects of Replacing the U.S. Income Tax with a Progressive Consumption Tax," paper presented at the North American Meetings of the Econometric Society, Chicago, August 31, 1978. See also Martin Feldstein, "The Welfare Cost of Capital Income Taxation," *Journal of Political Economy*, vol. 86, no. 2 (April 1978), pp. S29-S52.

When it is explicitly recognized that the present tax system involves an extra tax on corporate income as well as a personal tax advantage from retained earnings and that the value of the tax advantage is greater for investors having high personal incomes that are taxed at high rates, the accuracy of the estimates of the efficiency cost of the corporation income tax must be further qualified. It is assumed in all those estimates that the present tax system increases the cost of capital to corporations; Feldstein and Slemrod, however, have shown that it is possible for the combined effect of the corporate income tax and the exemption of retentions from current personal income taxes to decrease the cost of capital to corporations.[15] This comes about if investors having high incomes, to whom the exemption of personal taxes on retentions is particularly important, invest heavily in the corporate sector because of that exemption. As a result, even in the presence of a corporation income tax, there may be too much capital in the corporate sector, and reducing that tax might lead to greater inefficiency.

There are three important lessons to be drawn from the analysis of Feldstein and Slemrod. First, since the possibility that the result given by their analysis will actually arise depends on certain aspects of the behavior of individual investors in making up their portfolios, much more needs to be known about that behavior if the efficiency effects of the corporation income tax are to be understood. Second, since the result also depends on the preferential personal tax treatment of retentions, analyses of the cost of the corporation income tax must include explicit calculations of the costs of changes in that tax rate in the presence of other capital tax differentials rather than rely upon estimates of the gains made from equalization of all capital income taxes. Third, in an overall analysis of the inefficiency of the tax in a static economy, not only must the misallocation of capital be considered, but also the distortion in risk taking indicated by the tax-induced changes in the balance between corporate and noncorporate capital in the portfolios of investors.

These three points, along with the argument given earlier as to the importance of taking into account distortions other than those caused by taxes in assessing the welfare cost of the corporation income tax, indicate the tentative nature of present estimates of that cost. Nonetheless, on the basis of current studies of the effects of the corporation income tax in a static economy, it is probably safe to

---

[15] Martin Feldstein and Joel Slemrod, "Personal Taxation, Portfolio Choice, and the Effect of the Corporation Income Tax," National Bureau of Economic Research working paper no. 241 (April 1978).

conclude that from the standpoint of efficiency that tax is not a particularly attractive source of finance. As will become clear in the discussion in the next section, the effects of the tax in a growing economy reinforce this conclusion.[16]

Dynamic Inefficiency and the Corporation Income Tax

The corporation income tax almost certainly reduces investment. At a time when there is growing concern over the relatively low level of savings in the United States, this tendency of the corporation income tax to decrease savings, and thus investment, must be recognized.[17] In the general discussion concerning the adequacy of the level of savings in the United States and "capital shortages," some analysts have specified certain social goals—such as energy independence or pollution abatement—as having the highest priority and have then attempted to determine whether those goals can be achieved by a certain date at the present level of capital formation. Others have followed the more traditional positive approach—as opposed to the normative approach—in which the standard by which the level of current savings is judged is simply the efficiency or inefficiency of the rate of capital formation.[18] In this discussion of the cost imposed on society by the corporation income tax, we will follow the positive approach and assess the effect of the tax on the efficiency of the rate of capital formation in the United States. It is necessary first to clarify the meaning of an efficient level of capital accumulation, however.

The level of capital accumulation is efficient if the rate at which individuals are willing to trade present consumption for future con-

---

[16] Since virtually any tax causes some inefficiency, the inefficiency caused by whatever tax might be used in place of the corporation income tax must be taken into account in a final evaluation of the corporate tax with respect to efficiency. In the final section of this chapter, the estimates of the excess burden of the corporate income tax in a growing economy will be compared with some rough estimates of the inefficiency caused by other taxes.

[17] A review of the discussion of the adequacy of savings in the United States and the effect of government on savings is given by George M. von Furstenberg and Burton G. Malkiel in "The Government and Capital Formation: A Survey of Recent Issues," *Journal of Economic Literature*, vol. 15 (September 1977), pp. 835-78.

[18] These two approaches are contrasted in three papers presented at the 1976 meetings of the American Economic Association. Beatrice N. Vaccara, "Some Reflections on Capital Requirements for 1980," *American Economic Review*, vol. 67 (February 1977), pp. 122-27, takes a normative approach; Robert Eisner and Martin Feldstein argue for the positive approach. See Robert Eisner, "Capital Shortage: Myth and Reality," *American Economic Review*, vol. 67 (February 1977), pp. 110-15; and Martin Feldstein, "Does the U.S. Save Too Little?" *American Economic Review*, vol. 67 (February 1977), pp. 116-21.

sumption is equal to the rate at which the economy can make that trade. Clearly, if individuals are just indifferent as to whether they enjoy $1.00 worth of current consumption or $1.50 worth of consumption ten years hence, yet the economy is sufficiently productive that $1.00 worth of current investment can produce $2.00 worth of consumption goods in ten years, then there is a suboptimal level of savings, and a social gain can be made if individuals will save—that is, will invest—more in order to receive more future consumer goods.[19]

A utility-maximizing person will adjust the timing of his consumption so that the rate at which he is just willing to trade present consumption for future consumption is equal to the after-tax real interest rate that he receives. On the other hand, the rate at which society can make that tradeoff is determined by the marginal productivity of new investment. Therefore, any government policies that cause the after-tax rate of interest to diverge from the marginal productivity of new investment will cause inefficiency. Taxes on capital income will have just this effect. The cost of capital to firms is the before-tax return that they must pay to investors; consequently, firms invest to the point at which the marginal productivity of new capital is equal to that before-tax return. The tax acts as a wedge between the net rate of interest that is relevant to the savings decisions of individual investors and the return on new investment.

In the United States, the corporation income tax and the personal income tax together drive a tax wedge between the productivity of new investment and the return to savers. Feldstein and Summers have calculated the potential return on new corporate investment between 1946 and 1975 as having been roughly 12 percent.[20] If the value of the corporate tax rate is taken to be 40 percent and 30 percent is taken as the value of the marginal personal income tax rate, then the 12 percent return on new corporate investment corresponds to an after-tax return to savers of only 5 percent. This tax wedge is a very large distortion.[21] Removing this distortion would require doing away with

---

[19] As stressed by Feldstein, a rigorous description of the inefficiency discussed in the text should be focused on the distortion in the timing of consumption, not on a distortion in the level of savings. While we will occasionally refer to an inefficient level of savings, the estimates of this inefficiency discussed below will be based on the rigorous approach outlined by Feldstein. See Feldstein, "The Welfare Cost of Capital Income Taxation."

[20] Martin Feldstein and Lawrence Summers, "The Rate of Profit: Falling or Cyclical," *Brookings Papers on Economic Activity 1: 1977*, pp. 211-28. The average net return calculated for the entire period is 12.4 percent, while for the period 1966-1975 it is 11.2 percent.

[21] In this numerical example property taxes are ignored. Since they are taxes on capital income, those taxes exacerbate the tax wedge discussed in the text.

both the corporation income tax and the personal tax on capital income. One way to do this would be to substitute a tax on expenditures for the corporate and personal income taxes. Whether just such a tax change is desirable has been a subject of considerable controversy.[22] Without switching entirely to expenditure taxation, reducing or abolishing the corporation income tax would reduce this distortion and bring a gain in welfare to society.

While the general principle of the nature of the distortion arising from the taxation of capital income has been understood for some time, it is only in the late 1970s that the proper way of measuring the welfare cost of that distortion has been presented. Feldstein has shown that a calculation of the welfare cost of a capital income tax is based not on the reduction in savings caused by a tax on the return to savings, but instead on the reduced level of future consumption induced by that tax.[23] The two are by no means the same. Suppose, for example, that an increase in a tax on capital income causes a decrease in the after-tax interest rate; then, even if savings do not decline, future consumption must. One way of seeing this in the constant savings case is to note that the reduced rate of interest on constant savings reduces the consumption expenditures that can be made in the future. More generally—and more precisely—a decline in the interest rate raises the price of future consumption in present consumption forgone.[24] The utility-maximizing consumer will respond by reducing future consumption.[25]

Using a formula based on the distortion in the timing of consumption, Feldstein calculated the dynamic welfare cost of the corporation income tax as being about 0.5 percent of national income.[26] This calculation was based on the assumption that the rate of savings is not affected by changes in the return on savings. Feldstein indicated

---

[22] See, for example, W. D. Andrews, "Consumption-Type or Cash Flow Personal Income Taxation," *Harvard Law Review*, vol. 87 (April 1974), pp. 1113-88; Martin Feldstein, "Taxing Consumption," *New Republic* (February 28, 1976); and U.S. Dept. of the Treasury, *Blueprints for Basic Tax Reform* (Washington, D.C., 1977).

[23] Feldstein, "The Welfare Cost of Capital Income Taxation," pp. S34-S35.

[24] For example, at an interest rate of 10 percent, $1.00 of consumption next year costs about $0.90 today. If the interest rate falls to 5 percent, the price today of $1.00 of consumption next year rises to $0.95.

[25] For measuring the welfare cost of the tax wedge, the relevant consumer response to this price change is his income-compensated response. See Feldstein, "The Welfare Cost of a Capital Income Tax," pp. S40-S41.

[26] Ibid., p. S48. As is true of the estimates of the static efficiency cost of the tax, this estimate gives an annual welfare cost. This estimate is sensitive to the value of the tax rates in the economy. For a reasonable range of possible tax rates, the loss ranges from 0.35 percent of national income to 0.7 percent.

that he suspects that there is in fact a positive relationship between savings and interest rates, a suspicion borne out by the results of Boskin's study.[27] If savings are not constant, but instead they decline when interest rates decline, then the distortion in the timing of consumption is larger and, consequently, the welfare cost of the tax is greater than 0.5 percent of national income. On the other hand, if, as has been found in some studies, rates of saving increase when interest rates decline, then the welfare cost will be less than 0.5 percent of national income.[28]

The closeness of Feldstein's estimate of the welfare cost of the tax to the estimates discussed in the preceding section is only coincidental. The preceding section dealt with estimates of the cost of the intersectoral misallocation of capital in a static economy. In such static models there is no future consumption. The intertemporal inefficiency of corporate taxes must therefore be ignored when such a model is used. By using a growth model, Feldstein could attempt to measure the cost of the intertemporal inefficiency of the corporation income tax. However, he used a one-sector model in which it is assumed that all firms are corporations; consequently, his estimates do not include the cost of the intersectoral misallocation of capital.

It is tempting simply to add the intersectoral efficiency cost estimates to the intertemporal estimates in order to achieve an overall approximation of the welfare cost of the corporation income tax. As Feldstein pointed out, however, this is in general not appropriate.[29] An estimate of the cost of the combined intersectoral and intertemporal distortions of a corporation income tax must be derived from a model of a growing economy with at least one corporate sector and one noncorporate sector. Little work has been done using such a model, and that which has been done has produced conflicting results.

The simplest model capable of dealing with both the intersectoral and intertemporal distortions caused by a corporation income tax is a two-sector growth model. Use of such a model indicates that the gain in welfare from reducing the tax on capital in the corporate sector to the same level as the tax on capital in the noncorporate sector is equal

---

[27] Ibid., p. S44; Boskin, "Taxation, Saving, and the Rate of Interest."

[28] In a number of studies, Warren Weber has found a negative relationship between savings and interest rates. See, for example, Warren Weber, "Interest Rates, Inflation, and Consumer Expenditure," *American Economic Review*, vol. 65 (December 1975), pp. 843-58; see also the discussion of studies of interest rates and savings in von Furstenberg and Malkiel, "The Government and Capital Formation," pp. 840-42.

[29] Feldstein, "The Welfare Cost of Capital Income Taxation," p. S47, note 42.

to about 0.5 percent to 1 percent of national income if savings are unaffected by changes in the interest rate.[30] If savings are affected by changes in the interest rate—in particular if the elasticity of savings with respect to the interest rate is 0.4 percent, as Boskin estimated— then the loss of welfare is equal to between 1.6 percent and 2.3 percent of national income. This last set of figures is extremely large and indicates that the excess burden of the high tax on corporate capital income may be equal to as much as 70 to 75 percent of the revenues generated by that tax differential.

One of the reasons these estimates are so large is that both the extra tax on corporate capital income and a general tax on all capital income representing U.S. property taxes and personal income taxes are explicitly taken into account. Property taxes and personal income taxes drive a wedge between the return on new investment and the rate of interest received by investors. In the presence of those taxes, and even without a corporation income tax, the level of capital formation would be inefficiently low. The corporation income tax not only induces an intersectoral misallocation of capital and an intertemporal misallocation of consumption of corporate output, it also aggravates the loss of welfare arising from the general tax on capital income. If savings rates are elastic with respect to the interest rate, the corporate tax causes a significant decline in investment by reducing the return to capital. It is this decline in investment that reduces the already low level of capital formation for which the general capital income tax is responsible. This explains the very high estimates of welfare loss obtained through the use of Boskin's estimate of the elasticity of savings.

In the analysis that gives rise to these large estimates of the welfare cost of the corporation income tax, the method by which the loss in tax revenues is recouped is ignored. This can be quite misleading, since the tax that is used to make up the lost revenues is almost certain to cause some inefficiency, thereby offsetting, at least in part, the gain in welfare realized by removing the high tax on corporate profits. Fullerton, Shoven, and Whalley have investigated the effect of abolishing the personal income tax and imposing an expenditure tax instead.[31] As noted earlier, abolishing the income tax

---

[30] J. Gregory Ballentine, "The Cost of the Inter-sectoral and Inter-temporal Price Distortions of a Corporation Income Tax" (Detroit: Wayne State University, 1978), processed.

[31] Don Fullerton, John Shoven, and John Whalley, "General Equilibrium Impacts of Replacing the U.S. Income Tax with a Progressive Consumption Tax," paper presented at the North American Meetings of the Econometric Society, Chicago, August 31, 1978.

removes the tax on capital income and thus removes the distortion of savings decisions. Imposing a tax on expenditures for consumption, however, causes a distortion in the decision with respect to labor or leisure—a distortion that arises because the tax drives a wedge between the social cost of extra output in reduced leisure and the cost to an individual, which is the social cost plus the expenditure tax. An income tax causes the same kind of distortion, but when an expenditure tax is substituted for an income tax, the distortion is increased. Fullerton, Shoven, and Whalley found the overall effect of this tax substitution to be a loss, not a gain, in welfare.

The results achieved by Fullerton, Shoven, and Whalley do not directly apply to the potential effects of reducing the corporation income tax; however, if the loss of revenue caused by reducing that tax is made up through increased personal income taxes, then that change in the tax will also bring about a reduction of the savings distortion and an increase in the labor-leisure distortion and may, therefore, decrease welfare rather than increase it. Before much confidence can be placed in such a conclusion, more work needs to be done. This is particularly true since the results arrived at by Fullerton, Shoven, and Whalley appear to contradict a theorem proven by Atkinson and Stiglitz.[32] That theorem shows that, under conditions similar to those assumed by Fullerton, Shoven, and Whalley, substituting a tax on consumption for an income tax must increase welfare. The source of the discrepancy between the numerical estimates and the theorem is not clear, though there are a number of possible explanations. One important factor may be the fact that the expenditure tax considered by Fullerton, Shoven, and Whalley is not a pure expenditure tax. The base for the expenditure tax that they considered is simply the base for the U.S. personal income tax less savings. In view of the many exemptions and deductions that are available in the present personal income tax, the tax base used by Fullerton, Shoven, and Whalley was far from the pure expenditure tax considered by Atkinson and Stiglitz.[33] Independent of this issue, Fullerton, Shoven, and Whalley have stressed that they view their

---

[32] Anthony B. Atkinson and Joseph E. Stiglitz, "The Structure of Indirect Taxation and Economic Efficiency," *Journal of Public Economics*, vol. 1 (1972), pp. 97-119.

[33] One other explanation for the different results may rely on interactions of the many tax distortions, such as sales taxes, included in the model used by Fullerton, Shoven, and Whalley, but which were ignored by Atkinson and Stiglitz. Or the difference may arise from the fact that Fullerton, Shoven, and Whalley did not allow for any growth in the population, while Atkinson and Stiglitz produced a more faithful model of a genuinely growing economy.

work as incomplete.[34] The principal lesson to be learned from that work so far is that in the final analysis of the gain in efficiency to be realized from removing any tax, the effect of whatever tax is used to make up the lost revenues must be taken into account.

Summers also investigated the welfare effects of removing all taxes on capital income and relying instead upon an expenditure tax.[35] His results differ significantly from those achieved by Fullerton, Shoven, and Whalley; in particular, Summers found that such a tax change produces enormous gains in efficiency—gains of as much as $150 billion a year. The main reason for this result is that Summers's model implies very high values for the elasticity of savings with respect to the interest rate. While Fullerton, Shoven, and Whalley used a value of approximately 0.4 for that elasticity, Summers used values ranging from 2 to 7. Such high values for the elasticity of savings do not appear to be consistent with recent empirical work, but, as Summers shows, they are implied by some plausible assumptions concerning life-cycle savings behavior. Without empirical evidence to confirm such high elasticity values, Summers's conclusions remain quite tentative. His analysis does point out, however, the pressing need for further empirical work on savings behavior in order to improve our understanding of the effect of the corporation income tax and other taxes on capital income.

An Overview

Thorough analysis of the combined intersectoral and intertemporal welfare cost of the corporation income tax in a realistic setting in which there are other distortions, some caused by taxes, some having other causes, is only now being begun. Several studies have been completed in which part of the welfare cost has been evaluated, or in which the attempt has been made to calculate the combined cost, but in the absence of other distortions. While there are exceptions, the range of numerical results is sufficiently small that a broad tentative conclusion seems justified. Specifically, the welfare cost of the tax appears to be equal to something like 0.8 percent to 2 percent of national income. The lower bound of this estimate is derived by simply adding the Harberger-Shoven estimate of intersectoral inefficiency to Feldstein's estimate of intertemporal efficiency cost under the

---

[34] Fullerton, Shoven, and Whalley, "General Equilibrium Impacts of Replacing the U.S. Income Tax with a Progressive Consumption Tax," p. 28.

[35] Lawrence H. Summers, "Tax Policy in a Life Cycle Model," National Bureau of Economic Research working paper no. 302 (1978).

assumption of constant savings.[36] If there is some positive relationship, however slight, between savings and interest rates, Feldstein's estimate is too low. The upper bound allows for a small positive relationship between savings and interest rates. It is based on the results obtained using the two-sector growth model discussed in the preceding section.

If the loss is actually equal to approximately 1 to 2 percent of GNP, then the corporation income tax is an extremely inefficient method of raising revenues. These figures imply that the excess burden of the tax is between one-third and two-thirds of the tax revenues. In contrast, Edgar Browning estimated the welfare cost of taxes on labor income as constituting 9 percent to 16 percent of tax revenues.[37] He also presented rough estimates to suggest that the welfare cost of excise taxes is equal to approximately 26 percent of tax revenues.[38] The added cost to society of using corporate tax revenues instead of revenues from some other tax is a very high price for whatever gains in equity might be achieved through reliance upon corporate taxes. It seems unlikely that other tax sources cannot be used to generate the necessary revenues with clearer, more desirable effects on equity and at a lower cost to society.

---

[36] The Harberger-Shoven estimate used in the text to derive this lower bound is 0.3 percent, not the 0.5 percent actually reported by Harberger and Shoven. The figure of 0.3 percent is a scaled-down estimate that reflects the smaller share of corporate tax revenues in GNP today than in GNP in the mid-1950s, the period covered by Harberger's data.

[37] Edgar K. Browning, "The Marginal Cost of Public Funds," *Journal of Political Economy*, vol. 84 (April 1976), pp. 283-98.

[38] Ibid., p. 297.

6

Inflation and the Corporation Income Tax

Inflation can alter effective income tax rates significantly even when there is no change in real incomes or in the tax laws. The most obvious inflation-induced change in taxation occurs when individuals are pushed into higher personal income tax brackets because of purely inflationary increases in their nominal incomes. For example, a person who finds that his before-tax income of $20,000 has risen to $22,000 when prices have risen 10 percent has received no increase in real before-tax earnings; nonetheless, because that person pays personal income tax at a higher rate on $22,000 than on $20,000, his real after-tax income has declined.[1] This increase in the tax rate occurs because the structure of the personal income tax is progressive and the rate brackets are defined in current dollars instead of constant dollars. Since the corporation income tax is primarily a proportional tax, there is no similar effect tending to increase the rates at which corporation income is taxed. With inflation, however, real corporate profits are not properly measured under the present tax laws.[2] Consequently, inflation can lead to large and arbitrary changes in the rates of real corporation income taxes as well as of personal income taxes.

A tax system gives a proper measure of business income if the real tax burden resulting from any given real transactions is inde-

---

[1] Essentially the same effect arises from the fact that exemptions, deductions, and other parts of the personal income tax code are written in current dollars.

[2] This is also true of the measurement of personal income for tax purposes. In particular, with inflation taxable capital gains include purely inflationary gains in addition to real gains. A number of authors have discussed this problem. See, in particular, Roger E. Brinner, "Inflation and the Definition of Taxable Personal Income," in *Inflation and the Income Tax*, ed. Henry Aaron (Washington, D.C.: The Brookings Institution, 1976), pp. 121-52.

pendent of the rate of inflation.[3] For example, suppose that with prices stable a firm engages in certain real transactions and realizes a taxable profit of $1,000, on which it pays $500 in taxes. If, when *all* prices have risen 10 percent the firm engages in exactly the same real transactions, its taxable profits are measured as $1,100, and it pays $550 in taxes, then its real tax burden has not changed and the tax system has measured business income properly.[4] The tax system will give a proper measure of profits if all components of the revenues and costs of a firm are measured in current dollars or are all measured in constant dollars—that is, dollar values from some given earlier period. If some components of profits are measured in current dollars, however, and others are measured in dollar values from some earlier period, then the tax system will not give a proper measure of business income.

In the United States the sales revenues of a firm and certain costs, such as the cost of labor, are all measured in current dollars for tax purposes. However, some of the firm's costs are measured in dollars from an earlier period. Depreciation expenses are based on the historical cost of the firm's assets—that is, an asset that cost $1,000 and has a ten-year life for accounting purposes results in $100 of depreciation expense a year when the straight-line method of depreciation is used. This expense remains the same for ten years even if the general price level rises, thereby causing the replacement cost of the asset to increase.

Another component of costs that may be measured in dollars from an earlier period is the cost of materials. If a firm values its inventory according to the first-in, first-out method (FIFO), then the prices at which the materials used up in any given year are valued will be prices of some earlier period. If, instead, the firm uses last-in, first-out (LIFO) accounting and does not deplete its inventory of materials, then the cost of materials will be valued in current dollars. Even in the case of a firm using LIFO accounting, however, if some of the materials used up are not replaced in inventory, the materials used and not replaced will be valued at prices from an earlier period.

---

[3] This standard for properly measuring business income is based on Henry Aaron's definition of a "real" income tax system. See Henry Aaron, "Inflation and the Income Tax," *American Economic Review*, vol. 66 (May 1976), pp. 193-99.

[4] The qualification that the firm engages in the same real transactions is necessary because, in general, inflation may cause firms to engage in different real transactions. If two situations in which the firm engages in different real transactions are compared, the firm's real income will usually be different in the two situations, and even under a proper tax system its real tax burden should be different.

An example might clarify the importance of the depletion of inventories when LIFO accounting is used. Suppose that in 1960 a firm is established and 100 units of an intermediate commodity—one that is used in producing the output of the firm—are purchased initially. Suppose that when the firm begins operation, new purchases of the intermediate good are exactly matched by the amount of that good used in making the firm's product—that is, suppose that the inventory of the intermediate good is maintained at exactly 100 units. If LIFO accounting is used, the value of the intermediate commodity used in each year that the inventory is maintained will be determined by the price paid for that commodity in the current year. Now suppose that in 1978 output and sales required more of the intermediate good than was purchased in 1978 and the inventory of 100 units was thus depleted to, say, 75 units. If LIFO accounting is used, the cost of the additional 25 units of the intermediate good used in 1978 is given by the price paid for that good in 1960.

A final part of the firm's profits that is effectively measured in constant dollars is the change in the value of the firm's net debt. If a firm borrows $1,000 that must be repaid in one year and during that year prices rise 10 percent, then the firm realizes a capital gain, since it can repay the loan in cheaper dollars. Essentially, the value of the liability of $1,000 declines to about $900 because of inflation. This capital gain is not included in the taxable income of the firm. Notice that the tax issue here does not depend on whether borrowers or lenders anticipate the inflation. If the inflation is anticipated and does not alter real transactions, then the market interest rate that firms must pay will rise sufficiently to offset their capital gains. Put another way, lenders will demand higher interest rates so that they will be compensated for their capital losses incurred because of their being repaid in cheaper dollars. If there are no taxes, firms will realize no net advantage from their positions as debtors when inflation is anticipated. Under the present tax laws, however, firms can deduct their entire nominal interest payments from taxable income but need not include as income their just-compensating capital gains. Consequently, firms benefit from present tax laws because of their positions as net debtors.

A specific algebraic example of the effect of inflation under present business taxes may help to clarify and summarize what has been discussed.[5] Measured in first-period dollars, the profits of a firm, π, are the difference between its sales, S, and the sum of the costs of labor, L, and materials, M, depreciation, D, and interest expense, which

---

[5] This example closely follows Aaron, "Inflation and the Income Tax," pp. 194–96.

is the product of the interest rate, i, and the net debt of the firm, B. Thus,

$$\pi = S - L - M - D - iB.$$

Suppose that in earlier periods prices have been constant but that in the current period all prices and wages rise by the proportion α. Further, suppose that this inflation is fully anticipated and that it has no effects on real transactions. This means that the interest rate rises to $i(1+\alpha) + \alpha$. The first term is the increase in the interest rate needed to keep real interest payments constant, while the second is the compensation to lenders for the decline in the value of the funds they are owed. Finally, suppose that the firm uses FIFO accounting. The taxable profits of the firm under inflation of α percent, π', are

$$\pi' = (S - L)\,(1 + \alpha) - M - D - [i(1+\alpha) + \alpha]B.$$

If taxable profits were properly measured in current dollars they would be equal to $\pi\,(1+\alpha)$. The difference between the actual measure of profits and the proper measurement is

$$\pi' - (1+\alpha)\pi = \alpha\,(M + D - iB).$$

This equation provides a nice summary of the discussion. Taxable profits are *over*stated because of the *under*statement of the costs of materials and depreciation. Taxable profits are *under*stated because the capital gains on the net debt of the firm are omitted from taxable income. The net effect may be to decrease or increase taxable income in relation to the properly measured level. Which occurs depends in part on the amount of debt held by a firm. A highly levered firm—that is, a firm with a high debt–equity ratio—may realize large untaxed gains. Another important factor, however, is the duration of inflation and the accounting life of the capital stock of the firm. The capital gains on net debt depend only on the rate of inflation during the current period. But the understatement of the costs of materials and depreciation depends on the total amount of price inflation between the period in which the inventory or capital asset was purchased and the current period. If inflation persists for some time, even highly levered firms may find that their real tax burden is increased.

Nicholas Tideman and Donald Tucker have investigated the question whether adjustment for inflation—that is, indexing—of the corporation income tax base will increase or decrease taxes of various sectors of the economy and of representative firms in the economy.[6]

---

[6] T. Nicholas Tideman and Donald P. Tucker, "The Tax Treatment of Business Profits under Inflationary Conditions," in *Inflation and the Income Tax*, ed. Henry Aaron (Washington, D.C.: The Brookings Institution, 1976), pp. 33-80.

The inflation adjustment that they considered increases the costs of materials and depreciation by the amount of the increase in the general price level and includes capital gains on net debt in taxable income. Thus their adjustment for inflation produces the proper measurement of business income. Tideman and Tucker showed that while there is considerable variability among firms, when inflation begins the taxes paid by a firm will in general be higher if the measurement of income is adjusted for inflation. But as inflation continues, taxes would be lower under an indexed tax base than under the tax base as it is measured at present. Indeed, even well after inflation has stopped, the adjustment for inflation decreases the taxes paid by a firm. This time pattern arises because initially the inclusion of capital gains on net debt in an indexed system dominates the other effects of indexing and thus makes taxes higher than they would be in a nonindexed system. Later, the proper calculation of the costs of inventory and depreciation in an indexed tax system makes taxes lower than they would be in a nonindexed system.

Tideman and Tucker do not take into account any changes in the policies of a firm that might be the result of inflation in the absence of a measure of taxable income corrected for inflation. In fact, under such circumstances many firms can be expected to switch to LIFO inventory accounting, which automatically corrects the measurement of the costs of materials for inflation and would therefore reduce the taxable profits of a firm during inflation. Further, to take advantage of the omission of capital gains in net debt, firms could be expected to increase their leverage. George von Furstenberg has shown that, when such changes in the policies of a firm are taken into account, the relationship between the rate of inflation and the effective tax rate on real profits is quite complex.[7] Indeed, he finds that in the very long run, under certain roughly plausible assumptions as to the number of firms that will ultimately shift to LIFO accounting and the increased reliance on debt finance, the effective corporate tax rate in an inflationary economy may well be lower than that in an economy with stable prices or an indexed tax base. For a considerable period

---

[7] George M. von Furstenberg, "Corporate Taxes and Financing under Continuing Inflation," in *Contemporary Economic Problems 1976*, ed. William Fellner (Washington, D.C.: American Enterprise Institute for Public Policy Research, 1976). Von Furstenberg does not consider how firms might alter their choices of physical capital assets so as to reduce the tax penalty resulting from use of historical cost depreciation in an inflationary world. Alan Auerbach has shown that with inflation, firms will choose assets that have a longer life in order to reduce that tax penalty by postponing the time at which assets must be replaced at inflated market prices. See Alan Auerbach, "Inflation and the Choice of Asset Life," National Bureau of Economic Research working paper no. 253 (July 1978).

after the onset of inflation, however, the tax rate in the economy with an indexed tax base or stable prices will be lower than that in the unindexed inflationary economy.

The articles by Tideman and Tucker and by von Furstenberg dealt with the effect of inflation on the tax liabilities of corporations. The effect of inflation on the *total* tax burden on the capital income of corporations—that is, the effect on the combined corporate and personal taxes paid out of corporate capital income—is less ambiguous than the effect on corporate taxes alone. This is because the tax-free capital gains on corporate net debt are matched by capital losses for holders of corporate debt, losses that are not tax deductible. The effect of such capital gains and losses on the overall taxation of corporate capital income depends upon whether the tax gains made by equity holders—who are the ultimate recipients of the capital gains—are greater than the tax losses of bondholders. If the losses of bondholders are larger than equity holders' gains, then inflation must increase the effective taxation of corporate capital income. In their study of the effect of inflation on capital income taxation, Feldstein and Summers found that the capital gains and losses on corporate net debt caused by inflation give rise to tax gains and losses that approximately cancel out.[8] As a result, the only effect that inflation has on the overall tax burden on corporate capital income comes about from the understatement of materials and depreciation expenses, and, therefore, inflation raises the real tax burden on corporate capital income. Indeed, Feldstein and Summers found that inflation increased the effective tax burden on the whole corporate sector by 54 percent in 1977. They also found that, because of differences in inventory accounting practices and in the durability of physical capital in different industries, effective tax rates were increased by markedly different amounts among the different industries.

Our immediate concern is not whether the corporation income tax should be indexed against inflation, nor are we attempting to assess the effects of any particular indexing scheme.[9] Studies of the effects of indexing are relevant here because they show that with the present

---

[8] Martin Feldstein and Lawrence Summers, "Inflation and the Taxation of Capital Incomes in the Corporate Sector," National Bureau of Economic Research working paper no. 312 (January 1979).

[9] Two proposals for indexing for inflation have been given considerable attention. One is presented by John Shoven and Jeremy Bulow in "Inflation Accounting and Nonfinancial Corporate Profits: Physical Assets," *Brookings Papers on Economic Activity 3: 1975*, pp. 557-611, and "Inflation Accounting and Nonfinancial Corporate Profits: Financial Assets and Liabilities," *Brookings Papers on Economic Activity 1: 1976*, pp. 15-57. Shoven and Bulow go beyond the

unindexed system of taxation, the current inflation has produced arbitrary and rather complex changes in the effective taxation of real corporate income. These changes are not uniform throughout the corporate sector but instead differ among firms employing varying amounts of debt finance, among firms that use FIFO inventory accounting and those that use LIFO, and among firms having very long-lived capital assets as opposed to those with short-lived assets.[10] It is important to assess the effects of inflation-induced changes in real taxation on the economy. What little work has been done on this issue is the subject of the next section.

The Effect on the Real Economy of the Interaction between Inflation and Taxes

Under certain circumstances, including the absence of taxes on capital income or an inflation-indexed tax system, fully anticipated inflation

---

indexation discussed in the text and propose that accrued gains on the *market* value of a firm's debt be taxed. An example may help to explain the difference between this gain and the capital gain on a firm's net debt (αB in the algebraic example presented earlier). Suppose that prices are initially stable and a firm has $1 million outstanding in long-term bonds that pay a coupon of $50,000 a year, giving a real interest rate of five percent. Now let prices rise 10 percent and suppose that they are expected to continue to rise at that rate. The capital gain on the firm's net debt in the first year is $(0.1)\$1,000,000 = \$100,000$. This is αB in our algebraic example. But if the real interest rate does not change, then the inflation will cause the nominal interest rate to rise to 15 percent; thus the market value of bonds paying $50,000 a year will decline to $333,333. The firm could buy back its $1 million in bonds for $333,333, thereby realizing a capital gain of $666,667. It is this capital gain, whether realized or not, that Shoven and Bulow argue should be included in taxable income. This proposal has drawn considerable criticism. It has been pointed out that the initial decline in market value would be wiped out as the bonds approached maturity and were redeemed at their face value—$1 million in this example. Further, the capital gains realized by firms are matched by the losses of individual bondholders. Consistency would require that those accrued losses and the later gains realized as market values rose to the redemption value be included in taxable personal incomes. This would greatly complicate the taxation of personal income.

A more limited and more practical proposal is presented by William Fellner, Kenneth W. Clarkson, and John H. Moore in *Correcting Taxes for Inflation* (Washington, D.C.: American Enterprise Institute for Public Policy Research, 1975). In their proposal the capital gains and losses on changes in the market value of debt are ignored. Further, they propose cancelling the gain on the value of the firm's net debt (αB) against the undervaluation of inventory and physical capital that is financed by debt. Thus, under their scheme, only the fraction of the costs of materials and depreciation that is financed by equity would be adjusted for inflation.

[10] Though Auerbach did not examine the issue explicitly, his analysis showed that firms whose assets have shorter lives bear a greater tax burden because of the use of historical cost depreciation in an inflationary world. See Auerbach, "Inflation and the Choice of Asset Life."

will leave the real interest rate unchanged, causing the nominal rate of interest to increase by approximately the rate of inflation. If there are unindexed taxes paid on capital income, however, the after-tax real return will be reduced by inflation, even if the nominal rate of interest rises enough to keep the before-tax real return constant. For example, suppose that in the absence of inflation the real before-tax return on capital is 5 percent and a tax of 50 percent is paid on that return giving an after-tax real return of 2.5 percent. With a 10 percent rate of inflation, let the nominal before-tax return rise to 15 percent, leaving the real before-tax return unchanged at 5 percent. An individual paying taxes on the nominal return of 15 percent receives a nominal return of 7.5 percent after taxes, which implies that the real after-tax return is −2.5 percent. Thus, although there is no change in the tax rate, but because there is an unindexed tax system, the real return on savings declines. This is likely to reduce the level of real savings and, consequently, to reduce real investment in the economy.

In our example the nominal before-tax rate of interest was simply assumed to rise by the rate of inflation. Whether this actually happens is a complex question. If the nominal rate rises by more than the inflation rate, then the real after-tax return may not decline and, consequently, investment may not be reduced. Feldstein, Green, and Sheshinski have investigated this issue using a one-sector model of a growing economy.[11] They ignored the disequilibrium effects of unanticipated changes in the rate of inflation and instead concentrated on the long-run differences in real returns between those in an economy in which there is no inflation and those in one in which the rate of inflation is constant. Thus their results do not refer to temporary adjustments, but to the permanent effects of inflation when taxes are unindexed.

An important aspect of the analysis of Feldstein, Green, and Sheshinski is their inclusion of both debt finance and equity finance.[12] Under the present tax system, the effect of inflation on the net return on equity is not the same as its effect on debt. To abstract from changes in risk premiums, suppose that the aggregate debt–equity ratio

11 Martin Feldstein, Jerry Green, and Eytan Sheshinski, "Inflation and Taxes in a Growing Economy with Debt and Equity Finance," Journal of Political Economy, vol. 86, no. 2 (April 1978), pp. S53-S70.

12 In earlier articles those authors examined these issues in an economy in which all finance was by means of debt. See Martin Feldstein, "Inflation, Income Taxes and the Rate of Interest: A Theoretical Analysis," American Economic Review, vol. 66 (December 1976), pp. 809-20; Jerry Green and Eytan Sheshinski, "Budget Displacement Effects of Inflationary Finance," American Economic Review, vol. 67 (September 1977), pp. 671-82.

in the economy is fixed; then inflation necessarily causes the net real return on equity to decline because of the undervaluation of depreciation expenses on the basis of historical costs and because purely nominal capital gains on corporate stock are taxed.[13] Feldstein, Green, and Sheshinski found that under the present tax laws a rate of inflation of 10 percent will cause the net return on equity to decline by almost half.[14]

The effect of inflation on the real after-tax rate of interest is less certain. To see how the interest rate is affected by inflation, first suppose that the nominal rate of interest rises by the amount of the rate of inflation. Since individuals must pay taxes on their nominal interest earnings, this rise in the nominal rate of interest implies that the after-tax real rate must decline. (Recall the numerical example given at the beginning of this section.) However, since the nominal interest payments are tax deductible by firms, but the capital gains on the decline in the real value of their net debt are tax-free, firms will find that debt finance provides a tax advantage to them. Consequently, firms' demand for debt finance will increase and they will thus bid up the nominal rate of interest.

Because of the inflation-induced increase in the demand for debt finance, the real after-tax rate of interest will not decline as much as it would if the nominal rate of interest rose only by the amount of the rate of inflation; indeed, the real after-tax interest rate may rise. Suppose, for the moment, that depreciation expenses are correctly increased for inflation. Then the real after-tax rate of interest will rise if the corporate tax rate exceeds the personal tax rate and vice versa.[15] Essentially, the corporate tax rate indicates the size of the tax advantage of debt finance with inflation, while the personal tax rate indicates the tax disadvantage of a debtholder who is taxed on his nominal interest earnings. If the tax advantage of debt finance by a firm is greater than the tax discrimination against debtholders, firms will bid the nominal interest rate up so high that the real after-tax interest rate will rise. Obviously, since different investors face different per-

---

[13] Feldstein, Green, and Sheshinski abstract from intermediate goods—that is, goods used in the production of other goods. Thus firms do not hold inventories, and the valuation of the costs of materials is irrelevant. The debt–equity ratio is measured by the fraction of the physical capital stock that is financed by debt divided by the fraction that is financed by equity. Measuring the debt–equity ratio in this way avoids certain difficulties of measuring the monetary value of debt in an inflationary economy.

[14] Feldstein, Green, and Sheshinski, "Inflation and Taxes in a Growing Economy," p. S65.

[15] Ibid., p. S63.

sonal tax rates, the real after-tax rate of interest may rise for some investors and decline for others. In particular, investors whose incomes are high and who pay personal taxes at high rates are likely to find that their real net interest rate has declined as a result of inflation.

The understatement of depreciation expenses, which was ignored in the paragraph above, acts to reduce both the nominal and the real rate of interest. Since the capital stock is financed by both debt and equity, understatement of the depreciation of that capital stock for tax purposes has the effect of an additional tax on the income from both debt and equity.[16] Even when the corporate tax rate exceeds the personal tax rate, the understatement of depreciation expenses may cause the net real interest rate to decline. Feldstein, Green, and Sheshinski found that a 10 percent rate of inflation will cause the real after-tax interest rate for investors in the 50 percent marginal income tax bracket to fall from 2 percent to −0.7 percent. For investors in the 30 percent income tax bracket, the real net interest rate is virtually unchanged by inflation, while for those who pay no income taxes the interest rate doubles.[17]

Feldstein and Summers provided an econometric analysis of the effect of inflation on the real interest rate that confirms the general conclusions of Feldstein, Green, and Sheshinski.[18] The econometric results, however, show that inflation reduces the real interest rate for virtually all investors. Feldstein and Summers explicitly recognized that there are two competing effects on interest rates. The first is the inflation-induced tax advantage to firms as debtors. As discussed, this

---

[16] That is, even with debt finance, if a firm cannot deduct its true replacement cost as depreciation expense, the cost of an investment project is increased. For example, suppose that a firm is considering a debt-financed investment project that will bring a gross return of 10 percent, 3 percent of which is true depreciation. If the interest rate is 7 percent and the firm can deduct its true depreciation expenses, then the firm will be indifferent about the project. Suppose, however, that the firm is only allowed to deduct 1 percent of its true depreciation expenses. Then, if the firm pursues the project, the firm can deduct from the 10 percent gross return depreciation expenses of only 1 percent plus the 7 percent in interest payments. The remaining 2 percent return will be treated as profit and will be subject to the corporation income tax. If that tax rate is 50 percent, then the total cost of the investment will be 7 percent in interest payments plus 3 percent in true depreciation expenses plus 1 percent in extra corporate profits taxes because of the 2 percent understatement of depreciation expenses. Consequently, the understatement of depreciation expenses imposes an extra tax cost on the investment so that the total cost is now 11 percent; thus the firm will reject the investment.

[17] Feldstein, Green, and Sheshinski, "Inflation and Taxes in a Growing Economy," p. S67.

[18] Martin Feldstein and Larry Summers, "Inflation, Tax Rules, and the Long-Term Interest Rate," *Brookings Papers on Economic Activity* 1:1978, pp. 61-99.

effect tends to increase the nominal rate of interest above the real rate by an amount that is greater than the rate of inflation. The second effect is the increase in the taxation of all capital as a result of the inflation-induced understatement of depreciation expenses. This effect tends to reduce the nominal rate of interest and the nominal return on equity. Using a time-series analysis for the United States, Feldstein and Summers tentatively conclude that these two effects roughly cancel each other and that the nominal rate of interest rises by the amount of the inflation rate. As the example at the beginning of this section showed, this implies a sharp decline in the real after-tax rate of interest. That decline in the real after-tax interest rate is likely to reduce savings, inducing the long-run adjustments in investment and growth that were discussed in Chapter 3. Those adjustments imply that the capital–labor ratio in the economy will decline, thereby reducing the wage rate, so that part of the burden of inflation caused by an unindexed corporation income tax will spread to labor. Further, the inefficiency resulting from the suboptimal level of investment attributable to the existence of a corporate income tax in an economy in which prices are stable will be aggravated by inflation unless the tax system is indexed.

Summary

A central theme of the first five chapters of this study is that the corporation income tax has complex effects that are felt throughout the economy. Its burden is not borne by any well-defined group, but is shared by all of us. It distorts the allocation of capital throughout the economy and the allocation of output between current consumption and investment for future consumption. These distortions induce potentially large, but at present uncertain, losses of efficiency in the economy.

These effects of the corporation income tax are reinforced by inflation. Effective tax rates are made to differ significantly among firms because of differences in accounting practices, differences in the ages of capital stocks, and differences in the degree of reliance on debt finance. Further, during periods of sustained inflation, effective corporate tax rates will change as firms change their accounting practices, the type of capital that they use, or their leverage. The resulting tax differences among firms and changes in taxes in the course of time, and the complex effects of such tax differences and tax changes, make it all the more difficult to argue that reliance upon corporate taxation as a principal source of revenue is an aid to meeting the equity goals of society. Further, the likely effect of inflation as long as the corporate tax remains unindexed is to decrease the return on new investment, which in turn is likely to decrease the level of new investment. This will aggravate the loss of efficiency that is a result of the suboptimal level of investment induced by the corporate income tax.

BIBLIOGRAPHY

Aaron, Henry, ed. *Inflation and the Income Tax.* Washington, D.C.: The Brookings Institution, 1976.

Aaron, Henry. "Inflation and the Income Tax." *American Economic Review,* vol. 66 (May 1976), pp. 193–99.

Anderson, Robert, and Ballentine, J. Gregory. "The Incidence and Excess Burden of a Profits Tax under Imperfect Competition." *Public Finance,* vol. 31 (1976), pp. 159–76.

Andrews, W. D. "Consumption-Type or Cash Flow Personal Income Taxation." *Harvard Law Review,* vol. 87 (April 1974), pp. 1113–88.

Asimakopulos, A., and Burbidge, J. B. "The Short-Period Incidence of Taxation." *The Economic Journal,* vol. 84 (June 1974), pp. 267–88.

Atkinson, Anthony B., and Stiglitz, Joseph E. "The Structure of Indirect Taxation and Economic Efficiency." *Journal of Public Economics,* vol. 1 (1972), pp. 97–119.

Auerbach, Alan J. "Wealth Maximization and the Cost of Capital." National Bureau of Economic Research working paper no. 254, 1978.

Auerbach, Alan J. "Inflation and the Choice of Asset Life." National Bureau of Economic Research working paper no. 253, 1978.

Bailey, Martin J. "Capital Gains and Income Taxation." In *The Taxation of Income From Capital,* edited by Arnold C. Harberger and Martin J. Bailey. Washington, D.C.: The Brookings Institution, 1969.

Ballentine, J. Gregory. "Non-Profit Maximizing Behavior and the Short-Run Incidence of the Corporation Income Tax." *Journal of Public Economics,* vol. 7 (1977), pp. 135–46.

Ballentine, J. Gregory. "The Incidence of a Corporation Income Tax in a Growing Economy." *Journal of Political Economy,* vol. 86 (October 1978), pp. 863–76.

Ballentine, J. Gregory. "The Cost of the Inter-sectoral and Inter-temporal Price Distortions of a Corporation Income Tax." Detroit: Wayne State University, 1978. Processed.

Ballentine, J. Gregory, and Eris, Ibrahim. "On the General Equilibrium Analysis of Tax Incidence." *Journal of Political Economy*, vol. 83 (June 1975), pp. 633–44.

Ballentine, J. Gregory, and McLure, Charles E., Jr. "Taxation and Corporate Financial Policy." *Quarterly Journal of Economics* (forthcoming).

Baron, David. "Default Risk, Homemade Leverage and the Modigliani-Miller Theorem." *American Economic Review*, vol. 64 (March 1974), pp. 176–82.

Batra, R. W. "A General Equilibrium Model of the Incidence of the Corporation Income Tax under Uncertainty." *Journal of Public Economics*, vol. 4 (November 1975), pp. 343–60.

Baumol, William J. *Business Behavior, Value and Growth.* New York: Harcourt Brace and World, rev. ed., 1967.

Bayer, A. A. "Shifting of the Corporation Income Tax and Various Theories of Firm Behavior." *Public Finance*, vol. 25 (1970), pp. 449–61.

Boskin, Michael J. "Taxation, Saving, and the Rate of Interest." *Journal of Political Economy*, vol. 86 (Supplement, April 1978), pp. S3–S27.

Boskin, Michael J., and Lau, Lawrence J. "Taxation and Aggregate Factor Supply: Preliminary Estimates." In U.S. Department of the Treasury, *1978 Compendium of Tax Research.* Washington, D.C., 1978.

Bradford, David F. "The Incidence and Allocation Effects of a Tax on Corporate Distributions." Princeton, N. J.: Princeton University, 1977. Processed.

Break, George. "The Incidence and Economic Effects of Taxation." In *The Economics of Public Finance.* Washington, D.C.: The Brookings Institution, 1974.

Break, George F., and Pechman, Joseph A. *Federal Tax Reform: The Impossible Dream.* Washington, D.C.: The Brookings Institution, 1975.

Brinner, Roger E. "Inflation and the Definition of Taxable Personal Income." In *Inflation and the Income Tax,* edited by Henry Aaron. Washington, D.C.: The Brookings Institution, 1976.

Brittain, John A. "The Tax Structure and Corporate Dividend Policy." *American Economic Review*, vol. 54 (May 1964), pp. 272–87.

Brown, E. Carey. "The Corporate Tax in the Short Run." *National Tax Journal*, vol. 7 (September 1954), pp. 240–41.

Brown, E. Carey. "Recent Studies of the Incidence of the Corporation Income Tax." In *Public Finance and Stabilization Policy: Essays in Honor of Richard A. Musgrave*, edited by Warren L. Smith and John M. Culbertson. Amsterdam: North-Holland Publishing Co., 1974.

Browning, Edgar K. "The Marginal Cost of Public Funds." *Journal of Political Economy*, vol. 84 (April 1976), pp. 283–98.

Browning, Edgar K. "The Burden of Taxation." *Journal of Political Economy*, vol. 86 (August 1978), pp. 649–72.

Bruno, Sergio. "Corporation Income Tax, Oligopolistic Markets, and Immediate Tax Shifting: A Suggested Theoretical Approach." *Public Finance*, vol. 25 (1970), pp. 363–78.

Cauley, John and Sandler, Tod. "The Short-Run Shifting of the Corporation Income Tax: A Theoretical Investigation." *Public Finance*, vol. 29 (1974), pp. 19–35.

Christian, Ernest S., Jr. "Integrating the Corporate Tax: Methods, Motivations and Effects." Research report prepared for Donaldson Lufkin & Jenrette Securities Corporation, New York, and reprinted by the American Enterprise Institute (Washington, D.C., 1977).

Cragg, John G.; Harberger, Arnold C.; and Mieszkowski, Peter. "Empirical Evidence on the Incidence of the Corporation Income Tax." *Journal of Political Economy*, vol. 75 (December 1967), pp. 811–21.

Cragg, John G.; Harberger, Arnold C.; and Mieszkowski, Peter. "Rejoinder." *Journal of Political Economy*, vol. 78 (July/August 1970), pp. 774–77.

Diamond, Peter. "Incidence of an Interest Income Tax." *Journal of Economic Theory*, vol. 2 (September 1972), pp. 211–29.

Donaldson, Gordon. "Financial Goals: Management vs. Stockholders." *Harvard Business Review*, vol. 41 (1963), pp. 116–29.

Dusansky, Richard. "The Short-Run Shifting of the Corporation Income Tax in the United States." *Oxford Economic Papers*, vol. 24 (November 1972), pp. 357–71.

Eisner, Robert. "Capital Shortage: Myth and Reality." *American Economic Review*, vol. 67 (February 1977), pp. 110–15.

Feldstein, Martin S. "Corporate Taxation and Dividend Behavior." *Review of Economic Studies*, vol. 37 (1970), pp. 57–72.

Feldstein, Martin S. "The Incidence of a Capital Income Tax in a Growing Economy with Variable Savings Rates." *Review of Economic Studies*, vol. 41 (October 1974), pp. 505–13.

Feldstein, Martin S. "Tax Incidence in a Growing Economy with Variable Factor Supply." *Quarterly Journal of Economics*, vol. 88 (November 1974), pp. 551–73.

Feldstein, Martin S. "Taxing Consumption." *The New Republic* (February 28, 1976).

Feldstein, Martin S. "Inflation, Income Taxes and the Rate of Interest: A Theoretical Analysis." *American Economic Review*, vol. 66 (December 1976), pp. 809–20.

Feldstein, Martin S. "Does the U.S. Save Too Little?" *American Economic Review*, vol. 67 (February 1977), pp. 116–21.

Feldstein, Martin S. "The Surprising Incidence of a Tax on Pure Rent: A New Answer to an Old Question." *Journal of Political Economy*, vol. 85 (April 1977), pp. 349–60.

Feldstein, Martin S. "The Welfare Cost of Capital Income Taxation." *Journal of Political Economy*, vol. 86, no. 2 (April 1978), pp. S29–S52.

Feldstein, Martin S.; Green, Jerry; and Sheshinski, Eytan. "Inflation and Taxes in a Growing Economy with Debt and Equity Finance." *Journal of Political Economy*, vol. 86, no. 2 (April 1978), pp. S53–S70.

Feldstein, Martin S.; Green, Jerry; and Sheshinski, Eytan. "Corporate Financial Policy and Taxation in a Growing Economy." *Quarterly Journal of Economics* (forthcoming).

Feldstein, Martin S., and Slemrod, Joel. "Personal Taxation, Portfolio Choice, and the Effect of the Corporation Income Tax." National Bureau of Economic Research working paper no. 241, April 1978.

Feldstein, Martin S., and Summers, Lawrence. "The Rate of Profit: Falling or Cyclical." *Brookings Papers on Economic Activity 1:1977*, pp. 211–28.

Feldstein, Martin S., and Summers, Lawrence. "Inflation, Tax Rules, and the Long-Term Interest Rate." *Brookings Papers on Economic Activity 1:1978*, pp. 61–99.

Feldstein, Martin and Summers, Lawrence. "Inflation and the Taxation of Capital Income in the Corporate Sector." National Bureau of Economic Research working paper no. 312, January 1979.

Fellner, William, ed. *Contemporary Economic Problems 1976*. Washington, D.C.: American Enterprise Institute for Public Policy Research, 1976.

Fellner, William; Clarkson, Kenneth W.; and Moore, John H. *Correcting Taxes for Inflation*. Washington, D.C.: American Enterprise Institute for Public Policy Research, 1975.

Friedlaender, Ann F., and Vandendorpe, Adolf L. "Capital Taxation in a Dynamic General Equilibrium Setting." *Journal of Public Economics*, vol. 10 (August 1978), pp. 1–24.

Fullerton, Don; King, Thomas; Shoven, John; and Whalley, John. "A General Equilibrium Appraisal of U.S. Corporate and Personal Tax

Integration." Paper presented at the North American Meetings of the Econometric Society, New York, December 28, 1977.

Fullerton, Don; Shoven, John; and Whalley, John. "General Equilibrium Analysis of U.S. Taxation Policy." In U.S. Department of the Treasury, *1978 Compendium of Tax Research*. Washington, D.C., 1978.

Fullerton, Don; Shoven, John; and Whalley, John. "General Equilibrium Impacts of Replacing the U.S. Income Tax with a Progressive Consumption Tax." Paper presented at the North American Meetings of the Econometric Society, Chicago, August 31, 1978.

Furstenberg, George M. von. "Corporate Taxes and Financing under Continuing Inflation." In *Contemporary Economic Problems 1976*, edited by William Fellner. Washington, D.C.: American Enterprise Institute for Public Policy Research, 1976.

Furstenberg, George M. von, and Malkiel, Burton G. "The Government and Capital Formation: A Study of Recent Issues." *Journal of Economic Literature*, vol. 15 (September 1977), pp. 835–78.

Goode, Richard. *The Corporation Income Tax*. New York: John Wiley and Sons, Inc., 1951.

Goode, Richard. "Rates of Return, Income Shares, and Corporate Tax Incidence." In *Effects of Corporation Income Tax*, edited by Marian Krzyzaniak. Detroit: Wayne State University Press, 1966.

Gordon, Robert. "The Incidence of the Corporation Income Tax in U.S. Manufacturing 1925–62." *American Economic Review*, vol. 57 (September 1967), pp. 731–58.

Gordon, Robert. "Incidence of the Corporation Income Tax in U.S. Manufacturing: Reply." *American Economic Review*, vol. 58 (December 1968), pp. 1360–67.

Green, Jerry, and Sheshinski, Eytan. "Budget Displacement Effects of Inflationary Finance." *American Economic Review*, vol. 67 (September 1977), pp. 671–82.

Hall, Challis, Jr. "Direct Shifting of the Corporation Income Tax in Manufacturing." *American Economic Review*, vol. 54 (May 1964), pp. 258–71.

Harberger, Arnold C. "The Corporation Income Tax: An Empirical Appraisal." In *Tax Revision Compendium*, issued by the Ways and Means Committee of the United States House of Representatives. Washington, D.C., 1959.

Harberger, Arnold C. "The Incidence of the Corporation Income Tax." *Journal of Political Economy*, vol. 70 (June 1962), pp. 215–40.

106

Harberger, Arnold C. "Efficiency Effects of Taxes on Income From Capital." In *Effects of Corporation Income Tax*, edited by Marian Krzyzaniak. Detroit: Wayne State University Press, 1966.

Harberger, Arnold C. "Taxation: Corporation Income Taxes." In *International Encyclopedia of the Social Sciences*, edited by D. L. Sills. New York: Macmillan and Free Press, 1968.

Harberger, Arnold C., and Bailey, Martin, eds. *The Taxation of Income from Capital*. Washington, D.C.: The Brookings Institution, 1969.

Haugen, Robert A., and Senebet, Lemme W. "The Insignificance of Bankruptcy Costs to the Theory of Optimal Capital Structure." *Journal of Finance*, vol. 33 (May 1978), pp. 383–94.

Howrey, E. Philip, and Hymans, Saul H. "The Measurement and Determination of Loanable Funds Savings." *Brooking Papers on Economic Activity* 3:1978, pp. 655–705.

Johnson, Harry, and Mieszkowski, Peter. "The Effects of Unionization on the Distribution of Income: A General Equilibrium Approach." *Quarterly Journal of Economics*, vol. 84 (November 1970), 539–61.

Jones, Ronald. "Distortions in Factor Markets and the General Equilibrium Model of Production." *Journal of Political Economy*, vol. 79 (May/June 1971), pp. 437–59.

King, Mervyn. "Taxation and the Cost of Capital." *Review of Economic Studies*, vol. 41 (1974), pp. 21–35.

King, Mervyn. *Public Policy and the Corporation*. London: Chapman and Hall, 1977.

Krauss, Melvyn B., and Johnson, Harry G. "The Theory of Tax Incidence: A Diagrammatic Analysis." *Economica*, vol. 39 (November 1972), pp. 357–82.

Krzyzaniak, Marian. "The Long-Run Burden of a General Tax on Profits in a Neo-classical World." *Public Finance*, vol. 22 (1967), pp. 472–91.

Krzyzaniak, Marian. "The Burden of a Differential Tax on Profits in a Neo-classical World." *Public Finance*, vol. 23 (1968), pp. 447–73.

Krzyzaniak, Marian. "Factor Substitution and the General Tax on Profits." *Public Finance*, vol. 25 (1970), pp. 489–514.

Krzyzaniak, Marian, ed. *Effects of Corporation Income Tax*. Detroit: Wayne State University Press, 1966.

Krzyzaniak, Marian, and Musgrave, Richard. *The Shifting of the Corporation Income Tax*. Baltimore, Maryland: The Johns Hopkins Press, 1963.

Krzyzaniak, Marian, and Musgrave, Richard. "Discussion." In *Effects of Corporation Income Tax,* edited by Marian Krzyzaniak. Detroit: Wayne State University Press, 1966.

Krzyzaniak, Marian, and Musgrave, Richard. "Incidence of the Corporation Income Tax in U.S. Manufacturing: Comment." *American Economic Review,* vol. 58 (December 1968), pp. 1358–60.

Krzyzaniak, Marian, and Musgrave, Richard. "Corporate Tax Shifting: A Response." *Journal of Political Economy,* vol. 78 (July/August 1970), pp. 768–73.

Lee, Li Way. "A Theory of Management and Its Implications for Capital Structure and Merger." *Southern Economic Journal,* vol. 46 (July 1979), pp. 107–18.

Levy, Michael E. "Professor Baumol's Oligopolistic Model and the Corporation Income Tax." *Public Finance,* vol. 16 (1961), pp. 366–72.

McLure, Charles E., Jr. "A Diagrammatic Exposition of the Harberger Model." *Journal of Political Economy,* vol. 82 (1974), pp. 56–82.

McLure, Charles E., Jr. "Integration of the Personal and Corporate Income Taxes: The Missing Element in Recent Tax Reform Proposals." *Harvard Law Review,* vol. 88 (January 1975), pp. 532–82.

McLure, Charles E., Jr. "General Equilibrium Incidence Analysis: The Harberger Model after Ten Years." *Journal of Public Economics,* vol. 4 (1975), pp. 125–61.

McLure, Charles E., Jr. "State Corporate Income Tax: Lambs in Wolves' Clothing?" U.S. Department of the Treasury, Office of Tax Analysis paper no. 25, March 1977.

McLure, Charles E., Jr. *Must Corporate Income Be Taxed Twice?* Washington, D.C.: The Brookings Institution, 1979.

McLure, Charles E., Jr., and Surrey, Stanley S. "Integration of Corporation and Individual Income Taxes: Some Issues for Corporate Managers and Other Groups." *Harvard Business Review,* vol. 55 (September-October 1977), pp. 169–81.

McLure, Charles E., Jr., and Thirsk, Wayne R. "A Simplified Exposition of the Harberger Model, Part I. Tax Incidence." *National Tax Journal,* vol. 28 (March 1975), pp. 1–27.

Mieszkowski, Peter. "Tax Incidence Theory: The Effects of Taxes on the Distribution of Income." *Journal of Economic Literature,* vol. 7 (December 1969), pp. 1103–24.

Mieszkowski, Peter. "Integration of the Corporate and Personal Income Taxes: The Bogus Issue of Shifting." *Finanzarchiv,* vol. 31 (1972), pp. 256–97.

Mikesell, John L. "The Corporation Income Tax and the Rate of Return in Privately-Owned Electric Utilities." *Public Finance,* vol. 28 (1973), pp. 291–300.

Modigliani, Franco, and Miller, Merton H. "The Cost of Capital, Corporation Finance, and the Theory of Investment." *American Economic Review,* vol. 48 (June 1958), pp. 261–97.

Moffat, William R. "Taxes in the Price Equation: Textiles and Rubber." *Review of Economics and Statistics,* vol. 52 (August 1970), pp. 253–61.

Musgrave, Richard, and Musgrave, Peggy B. *Public Finance in Theory and Practice.* New York: McGraw-Hill, 1976.

Myers, Stewart C. "Determinants of Corporate Borrowing." *Journal of Financial Economics,* vol. 5 (1977), pp. 147–75.

Oakland, William H. "Corporate Earnings and Tax Shifting in U.S. Manufacturing, 1930–1968." *Review of Economics and Statistics,* vol. 54 (August 1972), pp. 235–44.

Peles, Yoram C. and Sarnat, Marshall. "Corporate Taxes and Capital Structure: Some Evidence Drawn from the British Experience." *Review of Economics and Statistics,* vol. 61 (February 1979), pp. 118–20.

Penner, Rudolph G. "Uncertainty and the Short-Run Shifting of the Corporation Tax." *Oxford Economic Papers,* vol. 19 (March 1967), pp. 95–110.

Ratti, Suresh P., and Shome, Parthasarathi. "The Incidence of the Corporation Income Tax: A Long-Run, Specific Factor Model." *Southern Economic Journal,* vol. 44 (July 1977), pp. 85–98.

Reaume, David M. "Short-Run Corporate Tax Shifting by Profit-Maximizing Oligopolists." *Public Finance Quarterly,* vol. 4 (January 1976), pp. 33–44.

Rosenberg, Leonard G. "Taxation of Income from Capital, by Industry Group." In *The Taxation of Income from Capital,* edited by Arnold Harberger and Martin Bailey. Washington, D.C.: The Brookings Institution, 1969.

Schwartz, Eli, and Aronson, J. Richard. "Some Surrogate Evidence in Support of the Concept of Optimal Financial Structure." *Journal of Finance,* vol. 22 (March 1967), pp. 10–18.

Scott, James H., Jr. "The Theory of Optimal Capital Structure." *Bell Journal of Economics,* vol. 7 (Spring 1975), pp. 33–54.

Sebold, F. D. "Short-Run Tax Response in a Utility-Maximizing Framework." *National Tax Journal,* vol. 23 (1970), pp. 365–72.

Shoven, John. "The Incidence and Efficiency Effects of Taxes on Income from Capital." *Journal of Political Economy,* vol. 84 (December 1976), pp. 1261–83.

Shoven, John, and Bulow, Jeremy. "Inflation Accounting and Nonfinancial Corporate Profits: Physical Assets." *Brookings Papers on Economic Activity 3:1975*, pp. 557–611.

Shoven, John, and Bulow, Jeremy. "Inflation Accounting and Nonfinancial Corporate Profits: Financial Assets and Liabilities." *Brookings Papers on Economic Activity 1:1976*, pp. 15–57.

Shoven, John, and Whalley, John. "A General Equilibrium Calculation of the Effect of Differential Taxation of Income from Capital in the U.S." *Journal of Public Economics*, vol. 1 (November 1972), pp. 281–321.

Slitor, Richard E. "Corporate Tax Incidence: Economic Adjustments to Differentials under a Two-Tier Tax Structure." In *Effects of Corporation Income Tax*, edited by Marian Krzyzaniak. Detroit: Wayne State University Press, 1966.

Smith, Vernon. "Default Risk, Scale and the Homemade Leverage Theorem." *American Economic Review*, vol. 62 (March 1972), pp. 66–76.

Smith, Warren L., and Culbertson, John M., eds. *Public Finance and Stabilization Policy: Essays in Honor of Richard A. Musgrave.* Amsterdam: North-Holland Publishing Co., 1974.

Stiglitz, Joseph. "Some Aspects of the Pure Theory of Corporation Finance, Bankruptcy and Takeover." *Bell Journal of Economics and Management Science*, vol. 3 (1972), pp. 458–83.

Stiglitz, Joseph. "Taxation, Corporate Financial Policy, and the Cost of Capital." *Journal of Public Economics*, vol. 2 (February 1973), pp. 1–34.

Stiglitz, Joseph. "On the Irrelevance of Corporate Financial Policy." *American Economic Review*, vol. 64 (December 1974), pp. 851–66.

Summers, Lawrence H. "Tax Policy in a Life Cycle Model." National Bureau of Economic Research working paper no. 302 (1978).

Sunley, Emil M., Jr. "Effective Corporate Tax Rates: Toward a More Precise Figure." *Tax Notes*, vol. 4 (March 1, 1976), pp. 15–24.

Surrey, Stanley S. "Reflections on 'Integration' of Corporation and Individual Income Taxes." *National Tax Journal*, vol. 28 (September 1975), pp. 335–40.

Tambini, Luigi. "Financial Policy and the Corporation Income Tax." In *The Taxation of Income From Capital*, edited by Arnold Harberger and Martin J. Bailey. Washington, D.C.: The Brookings Institution, 1969.

Tideman, T. Nicholas, and Tucker, Donald P. "The Tax Treatment of Business Profits under Inflationary Conditions." In *Inflation and the Income Tax*, edited by Henry Aaron. Washington, D.C.: The Brookings Institution, 1976.

Turek, Joan. "Short-Run Shifting of a Corporation Income Tax in Manufacturing, 1935–1965." *Yale Economic Essays*, vol. 10 (Spring 1970), pp. 127–48.

U.S. Department of the Treasury, *Blueprints for Basic Tax Reform*. Washington, D.C., 1977.

Vaccara, Beatrice N. "Some Reflections on Capital Requirements for 1980." *American Economic Review*, vol. 67 (February 1977), pp. 122–27.

Warner, J. B. "Bankruptcy Costs, Absolute Priority and the Pricing of Risky Debt Claims." *Journal of Financial Economics*, vol. 4 (1977), pp. 239–76.

Weber, Warren. "Interest Rates, Inflation, and Consumer Expenditure." *American Economic Review*, vol. 65 (December 1975), pp. 843–58.

Whalley, John. "Discriminatory Features of Domestic Taxation Policies and Their Impact on World Trade: A General Equilibrium Approach." Paper presented at the North American Meetings of the Econometric Society, Chicago, August 31, 1978.

Williamson, Oliver E. *The Economics of Discretionary Behavior: Managerial Objectives in a Theory of the Firm*. Chicago: Markham Publishing Company, 1967.

Wisecarver, Daniel M. "The Social Costs of Input Market Distortions." *American Economic Review*, vol. 64 (June 1974), pp. 359–72.